ACCLAIM FOR

BRAIN SURGEON

NOMINATED FOR THE NAACP IMAGE AWARD FOR NONFICTION LITERATURE

"In the medical memoir genre, there are few things more beautiful than this book . . . Black has a wonderful book-side manner. He's humble, yet self-assured . . . If you're up for some unique drama or if you love a good memoir, you'll love BRAIN SURGEON. In fact, you may need your head examined if you miss it." —*Philadelphia Tribune*

"His story, coupled with harrowing accounts of a handful of his patients, is cleanly written, inspirational, and a superb fit for the times in which we live." —*Booklist*

"Considered by some to be the greatest neurosurgeon alive . . . It's comforting to know he's around the corner at Cedars-Sinai." —*Los Angeles* magazine

"BRAIN SURGEON is an inspirational book about true heroes—readers will marvel at Keith Black's achievements both as a doctor and as a man, and will be in awe of his patients' courage and will to survive."

—Denzel Washington

"Black reflects on his extraordinary life and career . . . He is equally skilled as an author, alternating incisive writing about incisions with his personal memoir, insightful and inspirational."

—*Publishers Weekly*

"This book is so tastefully intricate in terms of detail . . . With incredible grace and humility . . . the brilliant doctor explains the mystery and scientific wonder of intracranial surgery."

—*New York Amsterdam News*

"I often get asked who the best doctor is in the world for various ailments. Truth is, it's a hard question. When it comes to brain tumors, however, the answer is pretty clear: Keith Black. He is the doctor people find when all the other doctors have given up. He is *that* guy . . . And Keith, from one brain surgeon to another: Thank you for honoring our profession. Well done."

—Sanjay Gupta, MD,
chief medical correspondent, CNN, and
New York Times bestselling author of *Chasing Life*

"In the pages of this book you will become acquainted with the wisdom, experiences, and intuitive powers of Dr. Keith Black . . . a warrior who fights to allow his patients to continue to touch and experience the world, and to preserve the place within us that houses our very nature."

—Forest Whitaker

BRAIN SURGEON

A DOCTOR'S INSPIRING ENCOUNTERS WITH MORTALITY AND MIRACLES

KEITH BLACK, MD

with ARNOLD MANN

NEW YORK • BOSTON

This book is not intended as a substitute for medical advice of physicians. The reader should regularly consult a physician in all matters relating to his or her health, and particularly in respect to any symptoms that may require diagnosis or medical attention.

Grand Central Life & Style
Hachette Book Group
237 Park Avenue
New York, NY 10017

www.HachetteBookGroup.com

Printed in the United States of America

Originally published in hardcover by Hachette Book Group.

First Trade Edition: August 2011
10 9 8 7 6 5 4 3 2 1

Grand Central Life & Style is an imprint of Grand Central Publishing.
The Grand Central Life & Style name and logo are trademarks of Hachette Book Group, Inc.

The Library of Congress has cataloged the hardcover edition as follows:
Black, Keith.
Brain surgeon : a doctor's inspiring encounters with mortality and miracles / by Keith Black with Arnold Mann. — 1st ed.
p. cm.
Summary: "A compelling look at one man's journey into the inner workings of the brain."—Provided by the publisher.
ISBN: 978-0-446-58109-7
1. Black, Keith. 2. Brain—Tumors. 3. Brain—Surgery. 4. Neurosurgeons—United States—Biography. I. Mann, Arnold. II. Title.
RC339.52.B53A3 2009
616.99'4810092—dc22
[B] 2008046708

ISBN 978-0-446-19814-1 (pbk.)

Book Design by Charles Sutherland

DEDICATION

This book is dedicated to my daughter, Teal, and son, Keith, my two greatest achievements in life. To my parents, Robert and Lillian Black, the ultimate educators. To my friend and patient Johnnie L. Cochran, Jr., who fought so bravely against his brain tumor. To my donors, particularly Maxine Dunitz, the Brain Trust (Pauletta Washington, Dale Cochran, Keisha Whitaker, Gloria Mitchell, Angelia Bibbs-Sanders, Carol Bennett, Yolanda Parker, and KC Miller), the Marciano family, and the Mashouf family, who give so much of their vision and resources so that one day soon we will win the battle against diseases that attack the human brain. To my patients, past, present, and future, they are the true heroes, and to the doctors, researchers, and clinical staff on the front lines fighting to find cures.

CONTENTS

CONTENTS

FOREWORD

By Forest Whitaker

"What can we do?"

This was my mother's reaction when she was told of the tumor that had invaded my grandmother's brain.

"Where do we go from here?"

As my mother pondered these questions she was reminded of a magazine article she had saved years before. There was a surgeon on the cover who was described as the best neurosurgeon in the world. She had saved it for its historic value, since the man on the cover of this magazine was black. Now she proceeded to search through her things to find the clipping, and then she made a call to the hospital to see if she could speak with Dr. Keith Black.

The call resulted in a conversation that led my mother to move my grandmother from the hospital in her hometown in east Texas to the West Coast, and Cedars-Sinai Medical Center in Los Angeles. She felt comforted by Dr. Black's calm, clear voice and manner, as he described the surgery that would save my grandmother's life.

Dr. Black would go to the place that housed my

grandmother's consciousness with all the tools of the modern surgeon at his disposal. He would open the door of her skull, pull back the membrane that protected the spirit of my grandmother's brain, and enter this uncharted territory.

This was sacred ground, and in the operating room a sacred space would envelop everyone who moved forward into this territory with Dr. Black as they worked to remove the tumor that was attacking the chamber of my grandmother's soul. Dr. Black would enter quietly, like a thief in the night, silently removing the demons that would otherwise destroy the animating force that allowed my grandmother her speech, thought, and movement.

"It went well, we were able to remove the whole tumor." These words sent joy directly into my mother's heart.

Two years later, my grandmother would return to east Texas with the magazine clipping that my mother had saved and proclaim to those who saw it that "the sun rises and sets on Dr. Keith Black." She would return to her vegetable garden in her hometown, holding on to the indomitable spirit that thousands of others who had fought the demon with Dr. Black had shared.

In the pages of this book you will become acquainted with the wisdom, experiences, and intuitive powers of Dr. Keith Black. Here you will meet a man who is a protector of the human spirit, a warrior who fights to allow his patients to continue to touch and experience the world, and to preserve the place within us that houses our very nature.

INTRODUCTION

For me there are few things more beautiful in the universe than the human brain. Unlike any other organ in the body, our brain is the essence of what makes us human, our memories, our thoughts, our personalities—one hundred billion nerve cells, working in absolute harmony to allow us to see, to smell, to move, to understand, and to create. We have only begun to understand the marvel of this three-pound mass of gray and white matter. I have focused my entire professional life on learning about the brain. As a young medical student I aspired to solve the riddle of human consciousness, to demystify the interface between the mind and the brain. Now, as a brain surgeon, my life's work is to operate within this sacred territory, within the most complicated and delicate structure in the known universe. This book is about that work, the efforts of my colleagues and myself to rid our patients of tumors and other diseases that attack the brain, and our continuing struggle to extend the boundaries of research as we race to find cures to save the lives of our patients. This book is about our victories, and sometimes our defeats. But this book is also about the courage of our patients, some of the bravest people I know. Few things imaginable are more devastating than an illness that attacks the brain. Yet my patients fight their illnesses with incredible courage, many times against staggering odds. My patients are my heroes, and this book is also their story.

Keith Black, MD

BRAIN SURGEON

CHAPTER 1

Tiger Country

You number one!" William Tao exclaimed, abruptly standing up and throwing his hands over his head as I entered the examining room. Had he been a football referee, he would have been signaling a touchdown. As it was, there was the better part of an entire backfield in the room. The wealthy Hong Kong entrepreneur had brought with him an entourage of well-dressed relatives—his wife, his sister, his brother-in-law, and his son—and they had all crowded into the exam room. Like Mr. Tao himself, they stood to greet me and to shake hands.

"Before, I am scared," Mr. Tao said. "I never had operation in the head. Now I have known you and met you! Confidence! Success! Yes!"

His supportive family reveled in their patriarch's energy and positive attitude—and there could be no doubt that he was indeed a patriarch. William Tao had made a fortune in Hong Kong real estate. Retired for twenty years, he now divided his time between homes in Hong Kong and Los Angeles, with ample time for travel. “We go on a cruise every year,” he told me. “My wife likes shopping. Everywhere shopping. We travel all the time. We’ve been everywhere.”

Clad in designer jeans and a Gucci belt, William Tao was a short man of sixty-three, very fit and slender, with a handsomely coiffed head of salt-and-pepper hair. His command of English was pretty good; nevertheless, his sister or his son translated when things got complicated.

His tumor seemed to appear out of the blue, Mr. Tao told me. Before this, he had never been sick a day in his life. “Look!” he declared, standing before me. “I eat right, very little. Healthy. Twenty-nine-inch waist!”

Two months earlier, he had been en route back to Los Angeles from Vegas to attend his mother’s funeral. She had died suddenly, and he was very upset. He was her only son, and they were very close. “I used to call her every day,” he said sadly. His wife was driving, and he decided to roll down the passenger window and feel the wind on his face during the sad four-hour drive back to southern California. The next day he had a headache on the right side of his head; he’d never had a headache before. Believing the wind was the cause, he took an aspirin, but it didn’t go away. The next day the headache was still there, and the next. Then he lost his balance in what the family described as a “seizure-like” episode. His brother-in-law had broken his fall as his body hit the ground.

The following day, an MRI scan revealed what appeared to be a large tumor in his brain. I was scheduled to remove it in the morning.

"Do you have any questions about tomorrow?" I asked.

"No questions," he said. "Everything is good. I want to go all the way! Bad or good. Never mind. Get it out!"

I was relieved that he remained steadfast in his commitment to the surgery. It had been a long and frustrating journey just to get to this point—six weeks, in fact. There had been a lot of wavering and a great many delays after his MRI scan.

"Can I wait?" he kept asking.

My response was always a very firm no. Each time Mr. Tao asked to defer the operation, I would explain that it needed to be done as soon as possible, that there was no time to waste. Meanwhile, the tumor kept growing.

Mr. Tao's family had hoped that their Chinese naturopath would be able to cure him in a week. I have a sincere respect for non-Western medicine, and I understood the Taos' desire to seek a holistic cure, but everything in my medical training and experience told me that surgery was the proper course of action. I suspected that this was a particularly aggressive tumor, and the clock was ticking.

When I looked at the MRI scans, the news for William Tao did not look good. The tumor growing in the right temporal lobe of his brain appeared to be a glioblastoma multiforme (GBM)—the most malignant of all brain tumors.

The Grade 4 glioma, or glioblastoma multiforme, is an enemy I have known for a long time, and one that I no doubt will be battling for years to come. This tumor spreads through the brain like a wildfire, consuming critical brain tissue in its path. Under the microscope, the pathologist sees areas of necrosis, or dead cells, where the tumor has outgrown its own blood supply. This is the center of the wildfire, dying from lack of fuel, even as the tumor continues to expand aggressively outward from the perimeter, destroying more cells as it grows. A glioblastoma can double in size in fourteen days, which is why I repeatedly emphasized to Mr. Tao that surgery was urgent. If I was correct, any delay could negatively affect his prognosis.

On an MRI scan, the outer edge of a glioblastoma looks like the tightly packed ranks of an advancing army—solid sheets of tumor cells massed on a front and ready to charge into battle. Beyond that edge however, a fifth column of isolated tumor cells has already infiltrated distant areas of normal brain. For this reason, surgery is only the beginning of a counterattack against the glioblastoma; both radiation and chemotherapy generally follow. Until very recently, however, none of our standard medical treatments has been able to meaningfully improve the long-term survival of GBM patients. While patients with less aggressive malignant brain tumors can survive five, ten, fifteen years or more, an overwhelming percentage of GBM patients are not alive two years after their diagnosis. Median survival is just nine to fifteen months.

In neurosurgery, the term "debulking" is used to describe an operation to reduce the size of a brain tumor that cannot be completely removed. For a glioblastoma, a debulking procedure is all but futile. Talking about 60, 70, or 80 percent removal is pointless; even removing 90 percent of it would accomplish nothing. A tumor may have ten billion cancer cells; if I remove 90 percent of it, a billion cancer cells still remain. And a billion GBM cancer cells can multiply back into ten billion cancer cells within weeks—a glioblastoma grows back that fast. Anything less than an image-complete resection, where no visible tumor can be seen on the post-operative MRI scan, usually does little to extend the life of the patient. As a surgeon, I know that I must get 99.9 percent of the tumor out in order to have a significant impact on my patient's survival.

For now, this tumor almost always wins the war, and its victims are many. Before I met with Mr. Tao and his family, I had already seen three other patients with GBMs that week, and there would be more next week, and the week after that. My dear friend Johnnie Cochran succumbed to a glioblastoma in March 2005; Senator Edward Kennedy was diagnosed with one in May 2008. It is a grim and cruel irony that the deadliest of all malignant brain tumors should also be the most common. Of the 22,000 Americans diagnosed each year with primary brain tumors (those that start in the brain rather than elsewhere in the body), more than half will have GBMs.

This brutal truth weighs heavily on me every time I enter the operating room and face one of these highly aggressive tumors.

The time had come to walk my patient through the steps of his operation and his follow-up treatment. I kept my voice even, familiar. Recounting the risks of the operation with patients and their families was something I had done thousands of times before surgery. "The location of the tumor appears to be good," I said to Mr. Tao, "and I will do everything I can to keep the risk of your surgery low. So we expect everything to go very well for you tomorrow. Okay?"

"You are the best!" exclaimed Mr. Tao.

That is what the Taos' research had led them to conclude—that I offered them the best possible chance to save his life. It is what all patients turning their brains over to the care of a neurosurgeon want to believe—and what a lot of neurosurgeons believe about themselves. A neurosurgical colleague once said to me, "If you want to understand neurosurgeons, you have to realize that all neurosurgeons think they are the best in the world." There's a lot of ego among neurosurgeons, and it goes far beyond the length of time it takes to become one—four years of medical school, seven years of residency, and one or two years of fellowship training. It even goes far beyond any sense of elitism conferred by the reputation of the particular schools and medical centers where they have trained. Like fighter pilots, excellent neurosurgeons must have finely developed motor skills, pinpoint accuracy, and the ability to remain cool in high-risk situations. But the best of the best also have something more—the ability to empathize with their patients, and a well-developed appreciation for both the natural wonders and the natural dangers that are ever present within the brain.

Complicating matters for tumor patients in search of the best brain surgeon is the fact that the major focus of most neurosurgery in the United States is not the brain but the spine. Spinal fusions and disk repairs are the most common neurological operations, and of our 3,000 neurosurgeons, approximately 2,600 operate primarily on the spine. These neurosurgeons are likely to perform on average only a dozen or so brain surgeries a year.

Of the remaining 400 intracranial specialists—neurosurgeons who work regularly in the brain—each performing a hundred or more brain surgeries annually, half are vascular specialists. This means that they deal with aneurysms and other disorders involving the blood vessels of the brain. Still other neurosurgeons focus on the surgical treatment of epilepsy or on congenital brain disorders. That leaves only about fifty neurosurgeons nationwide who specialize in brain tumors. Of these, I am one of just a few who do more than 250 surgeries a year.

To be sure, a neurosurgeon who performs ten to thirty brain surgeries annually may still be able to get a good resection on a difficult tumor without causing the patient postsurgical deficits. That said, how well a surgeon knows his or her way around the brain, and whether or not he or she is able to remove a difficult tumor without causing paralysis and other serious deficits, is largely a function of experience. I believe that the experienced brain surgeon has better odds for achieving an image-complete resection without hurting the patient.

In my opinion, the minimum number of operations a brain tumor surgeon should be doing per year is fifty. A surgeon who performs fifty brain tumor surgeries annually will have enough experience to handle almost any situation that arises in the operating room. To carry the fighter pilot analogy a bit further, pilots who are flying once a month or once every other month are not going to be as proficient as the pilot who is up there four times a week. That's why the FAA demands certain standards in flying; that's why pilots must keep their hours up.

Even the relatively inexperienced pilot can fly an aircraft on a clear day. It's a different matter entirely if you are headed into a storm and need to land in bad weather—zero visibility, wind gusting at fifty miles an hour, rain blowing horizontally—and with mountains all around. Under these conditions, the pilot does not have time to read the manual and sort out how to make a safe instrument landing—and working in the brain is like that much of the time. Whether you're a pilot or a neurosurgeon, you've got to keep your hours up, especially if you're going to be doing complex and challenging surgeries like Mr. Tao's.

William Tao's surgery that morning would be fairly

straightforward, which did not mean that it would be easy. Operating in the brain is an adventure into a beautiful but unforgiving and potentially dangerous world. It is a trek through what I call Tiger Country. Every part of the brain has land mines and booby traps. If I get too close to the olfactory nerve, Mr. Tao will lose his sense of smell. If I damage the optic nerve, he will not be able to see; damage the third, fourth, or sixth cranial nerves, and he will have double vision. If I get too close to the facial nerve, his face will be paralyzed. Damage the hypothalamus and he will be unable to regulate his body temperature or fluid balance, and his endocrine functions will be lost. Bruise the brain stem and William Tao will never wake up.

I often liken myself to a thief in the night. Like an intracranial pickpocket, my job is to sneak into the brain and tease the tumor out, without the brain ever knowing I was there. It's like knowing the pathway into the secret chamber of the Great Pyramid. If you understand the anatomy of the brain, and you understand the principles of surgery in the brain, you can get into the chamber without releasing the demons.

My goal is to never touch the brain itself. The brain is sacred territory; it is not possible to manipulate normal brain tissue without unleashing the tiger, triggering the body's alarms and creating neurological deficits. But if I can be that perfect thief in the night, sneak in and snatch the tumor without touching the brain, the tiger remains asleep and patients like William Tao can emerge from surgery intact. They will then be able to live out the full span of their lives, or at least have more precious time to share with their loved ones. And that is why I do what I do—and why I want to share my story.

I want to take you into the operating room, where patients' lives are being saved and extended. I want to open the door to the research labs, where the war against the malignant brain tumor is being fought on a biological level. This book is a personal exploration of my development as a scientist and as a surgeon, and the challenges I confronted, both personal and professional, in order to enter the elite field of neurosurgery and make my contributions to it. Mostly, however, this book is about the patients whose stories provide its spine and soul.

The bravest people I know are not the doctors who undertake a great surgery and save or prolong a life. We are not the heroes; we are not the ones putting our lives on the line. The real heroes are the patients, who face their life and death challenges with the greatest of courage. Their stories reveal the true value of life, and the value of the relationships we share with our loved ones. Through my story and theirs, you will begin to understand our fight to survive, to live, and defeat the odds.

My colleague, neurosurgeon Dr. Geno Hunt, began the opening at 9:00 a.m., making the incision along the right side of Mr. Tao's head, peeling back the scalp, and cutting out a section of skull over the operative area. After he removed the skull section, he peeled back the leathery dura mater to expose the temporal region of Mr. Tao's brain. *Dura mater* is Latin for "tough mother," and it is the protective outer covering of the brain. By the time I was ready to begin the tumor extraction, the pathology results of the first biopsy specimens, taken by Geno, had come back from Dr. Serguei Bannykh, our director of neuropathology.

"It is a GBM," Geno confirmed to me as I approached the table. I had hoped I was wrong, but I was not surprised.

At 10:00 I started working on Mr. Tao's tumor, using the bipolar coagulator and suction, working around its borders, separating tumor from normal brain. This is always a very slow, methodical process. It is essential to know where I am in the brain at all times. The three-dimensional MRI navigation and intraoperative ultrasound are helpful; I use the image-guided MRI navigation to update the mental 3-D image of the tumor I keep in my mind as I work.

Gliomas can look almost exactly like normal brain, but after five thousand brain tumor surgeries, I've come to know what the enemy looks like, how it presents itself, and how it tries to hide. To separate out the tumor, I watch for slight differences between tumor and normal brain in color, texture, vascularity, and other factors. Tumors, for instance, tend to bleed more than normal brain tissue, because their blood vessels are fragile and break down easily when touched. Even though the tumor may look and feel very much like normal brain, it is often how it behaves to the touch that is the most telling. If I am extremely gentle and stroke the tumor lightly, as if with a feather, the tumor, because of its slightly different density, will begin to carve itself out from the normal white matter in the brain.

By 10:30 I had made my way down around William Tao's brain stem and was peeling the tumor off the arachnoid plane. The arachnoid plane is a membrane comprised of two layers of wet, transparent tissue. It is extremely thin—thinner than onionskin—and it was all that separated the glioblastoma from his brain stem. My strategy was to stay on the inside of that arachnoid plane and peel the tumor off that piece of membrane without perforating it, thus protecting the vessels on the other side. This was the very heart of Tiger Country, but I still had a great deal of confidence as I proceeded. As long as I could see that the thin membrane was intact, I was good to go. If I saw a hole in that tissue and started seeing that little lattice of micro-vessels, I would have backed out of there, like a pilot averting a storm front. Mr. Tao's surgery went smoothly, and at 11:03, I lifted the bulk of the tumor out of the excavation.

At 11:40, the tumor removal was complete. By this time tomorrow, Mr. Tao would be walking the Cedars-Sinai halls. Today it was his family members who were walking the halls, pacing the waiting area when I arrived.

"The surgery went well," I said to the family. "It turned out to be a tumor. It's what we call a glioma. It's a very aggressive glioma—a glioblastoma."

I could feel their hearts sink. "This is not the end of his treatment," I told them. "We can still get an increase in survival with radiation and chemotherapy, and perhaps the new vaccine we have in clinical trials."

The odds of long-term survival with glioblastoma are not good, but people with malignant brain tumors are grateful for any time I can give them. You might think that if you tell someone that he has only nine months or a year to live, he would panic and go into a major depression. My patients aren't like that. When they receive the news, they are naturally upset and grieve for themselves. They express concern for their families and other people they love and care for. And then, almost all of my patients choose to fight, even in the face of the most dire prognosis. If I can give them another six months or year of quality life, I'll do it.

Over the years I've learned that my patients are people who can live an entire lifetime in six months or a year. What they do with this time represents a much higher quality of life than that enjoyed by "normal" people who are caught up in the trivia of day-to-day, and not really focused on what is important. When you are given a year with the people you love, you don't squander the gift. You don't sit around playing video games or watching reruns—not if you have a young son or daughter with whom you need to build a relationship they will remember for the rest of their lives, or a spouse you might fall in love with all over again.

Very rarely do I see a patient who says, "I just want to give up and go off to Tahiti." My patients are fighters—

especially when they are given the tools they need to fight the best battle they can. I am in awe of their courage on a daily basis. And as long as they want to fight, I'll be right there in Tiger Country with them.

People often ask me, "How can you work with these patients, knowing that so many of them are going to die?" I cannot imagine better people to work with. I learn from them, as I watch them cherish every moment of their days. These people teach us all about the meaning of life well-lived. It is my hope that their lesson of life will come through in the pages of this book, and if it does, in whatever measure, I will have them to thank.

CHAPTER 2

A Love Affair with the Brain

Jell-O . . . custard . . . pudding . . . oatmeal . . . tapioca . . . sour cream . . . mayonnaise . . . cottage cheese . . . These squishy-spongy foods are often used to describe the consistency or texture of the brain.

Many of us have memories of being led blindfolded through a Halloween haunted house as a kid. The house had all the requisite spooky noises, eerie laughter, and creaking doors, but at some point in the tour, your guide (who maybe sounded a lot like your older brother) plunged your already trembling little hand into a fishbowl full of cold, clammy goop, and informed you that it was "brains." It was, of course, one of the common food substances named above, but your imagination was already working overtime, and the sudden sensation evoked the hoped-for shiver and the even more coveted "Eeeew-Yuck!" response.

Sadly, this reaction still occurs—not just in children but

in adults as well. Many people believe that because it is pale, soft, and gelatinous, the brain is somehow gross, or ugly.

Not me. I believe that the human brain is the most beautiful thing in the world. The anatomy I see during surgery is spectacular. It is elegant, not just on the surface but even more so beneath it, where after all my years as a neurosurgeon, I continue to marvel at how the various pathways integrate and twist with one another. To me, there is still nothing more exquisite in the universe than that.

For as long as I can remember, I've been fascinated by science and medicine, even as a small child. I was born in Tuskegee, Alabama, on September 13, 1957, and my earliest memories growing up in Auburn, Alabama, are of being out in nature. It was all semi-rural at the time, and I was five when I got a gallon jug from the school lunchroom and began collecting tadpoles from nearby streams. I kept them in jars in my room, which even then I considered my laboratory. I watched closely to see how they used their tails as an energy source, and even more intently over the days as they absorbed their tails and developed into little frogs.

Eventually I learned that I could anesthetize frogs with alcohol. I would simply put a cotton ball in front of their nostrils, and they would go under. Then I'd borrow my older brother's biology book, which had these great overlay transparencies of frog anatomy, and I would dissect the frog. My parents had already bought me a dissection kit. I would correlate the location of the frog's major organs—heart, lungs, spleen, liver, stomach, intestines—with the diagrams in the book, and then I would spend the longest time looking at the beating heart. It was all somewhat precocious—I was only about seven years old at the time.

I was constantly conducting experiments. I would tie strings to the legs of beetles and observe their aerodynamics while flying. A milk carton and a straw became a wind speed indicator. Held outside the window of my father's 1960 Buick, I could tell everyone how fast we were going within a few miles per hour.

I even got my friends involved. All of us in the neighborhood had BB guns; in Alabama, hunting was just something you did as a boy. My friends would shoot birds, and if one was still alive, I would rush it back to my little makeshift emergency room and try to save the bird's life. I'd try to get the BB out and close up the wound.

In today's society, a little boy who spends a lot of time cutting up frogs and birds might be considered borderline ghoulish, or a budding sociopath, but it was nothing like that at all. It was completely natural. My father recognized my experimentation as the genuine interest in medicine that it was, and did everything he could to encourage me.

Robert Black, my father, was and is the ultimate educator; he has always known how to take a child's natural curiosity and make it blossom into a quest for knowledge. He had a passion for teaching, and did it very well.

The tadpoles were pretty much his idea; he believed that young boys could learn more about science in the great outdoors than we ever would if we were cooped up in a classroom—and he was right.

At that time he was the principal of Auburn's all-black Boykin Street Elementary School, where he fostered the love of learning in his students just as he did with my brother and me. His devotion to quality education did not always sit well with the white power structure of the city: The reason my brother's biology book was so good was that my father demanded that the Auburn School Board supply his students with the latest textbooks, not the outdated hand-me-downs from the white schools that they had been accustomed to providing. Although his attempts to integrate the Boykin student body failed, he did succeed in bringing white teachers on staff, including a white librarian who taught French to fourth graders.

My father is a very scholarly man who as a boy developed what would become a lifelong appetite for books and reading. After combat service in the Navy during World War II, he earned his degree in elementary school education from the University of Alabama, and graduate degrees in school administration at the University of Pennsylvania.

For my father, life was never about the money. He judged himself not by what he achieved in life, but by what his children achieved. His goal for himself and for us was the pursuit of intellectual excellence. As a father he was a tough but compassionate taskmaster, debating my brother and me late into the night. "The best Black," he always told us, "is yet to be born."

My mother, Lillian, is the daughter of a sharecropper. She was the only one of her sisters to attend college, and taught first grade at Boykin Elementary. Like my father, she was dedicated to giving my brother and me the best possible start in life, even if it meant that both of them had to wear their shoes until the soles had worn paper-thin—or worse. "We were padding more sidewalk than leather in those days," she would later tell me. When my brother, Robert Jr., was old enough to enter high school, she never hesitated to spend every penny we had to send him to the Brewster Academy, a private boarding school in New Hampshire. Much as she missed having him around, she believed it was better to send him away than to handicap him for life with a second-rate education at Drake, Auburn's all-black high school.

My parents saw opportunities for learning in even the most common household tasks. Whenever my mother cleaned a chicken for dinner, she would give me the heart, which I would take out on the back steps and dissect, observing the chambers and the anatomy of the muscles and valves. Seeing how fascinated I was with a chicken heart, my father brought me home a turkey heart from the school cafeteria. One day he surprised me with a cow's heart from the slaughterhouse, which I carefully dissected. I spent hours investigating every aspect of this huge, multichambered mammalian heart. My father understood that I had a gift, and nourished it in a progressive educational format—chicken to turkey to cow.

John Locke said that you have to learn through the senses—you see it, smell it, taste it, hear it, and feel it. And that was surely the way I was taught: by experience, even if that experience was not entirely positive. Any transgressions in the pursuit of learning were quickly forgiven—including the day I blew up the kitchen. I was about eight years old at the time. My father had bought me a chemistry set, and I was in the process of heating some chemicals on the stove for an experiment—sulfur and a few other things—when all of a sudden flames shot out of the pot and the mixture exploded with a great flash and boom. The power of the blast threw me across the room. When I got the courage to open my eyes, I could see that my mother's immaculate kitchen was a shambles. The place was full of smoke, and everything—the stove, the kitchen table, the sink and counters, the walls and floors—was covered in soot, including me. It looked like a bomb had gone off, which, as I examined what remained of the pot, was not far from the truth.

Before I could begin cleaning up, I heard my parents pulling into the driveway. Frankly, I was glad they were home—I knew how close I'd come to really hurting myself. I went running out the kitchen door, waving my arms and yelling, "The kitchen exploded! The kitchen exploded!"

My father rushed into the house, fully expecting to find the place on fire. I followed, along with my mother. There they stood, surveying the wreckage, and me, the shamefaced guilty party. Even as I was trying to figure out why it had blown up, I waited anxiously for what I was sure would be the second detonation—my father exploding at me for what I'd done.

It never happened. "Been working with your chemistry set?" he asked calmly. That was it. No yelling. No scolding. Not even a slap on the wrist in punishment. Even my mother wasn't upset. What I had done, they'd realized immediately, had been done in the pursuit of learning, which was always an instant Get-Out-of-Jail-Free card in our family. Mom even helped me clean up. Such was my learning environment.

My parents knew that soon they would have to confront the same problem with me that they'd faced with my brother. There was no way they would enroll me in Auburn's less-than-mediocre segregated high school. They wanted me to go to college, and they wanted me to be able to go anywhere I wanted to go. This time they solved the problem for the family as a whole by finding new jobs. My father took a position as principal of an elementary school in the Cleveland suburb of Warrensville Heights, Ohio, and we moved to nearby Shaker Heights, which had an excellent high school. That fall, my mother would begin teaching at Scranton Elementary in Cleveland itself. At the end of the school year in June, we packed up the house in Auburn and she and my brother set off for our new home. I accompanied my father to the University of Pennsylvania, where he was taking graduate coursework toward his doctorate in education.

During the day, while he was in class, I roamed the campus, entirely unsupervised. I was ten. Not surprisingly, I gravitated to the school of medicine, where I wandered the corridors of the research labs, gleaning what I could by eavesdropping from the hall. Needless to say, I didn't exactly blend in. I soon became an object of curiosity to the researchers and doctors who worked there—this little black kid poking his head in various doors and windows—and they began inviting me in.

Those ordinary green buildings opened up a new world to me. I watched with great interest as a team of researchers conducted pulmonary function studies, measuring pulmonary resistance and lung compliance in human research subjects, and analyzing their blood gases. The researchers took the time to explain the purpose of their studies to me. During that summer, I drank in as much information as they would give me.

At least as much as the knowledge itself, however, I drank in their love for their work. I could feel their excitement—both for the intellectual pursuit of scientific discovery, and for their sense of pioneering exploration into the mechanisms of life. Their enthusiasm was positively contagious. At the age when some kids start to get the message that their life choices are limited, I didn't get derailed. These researchers opened up my possibilities, and reinforced the encouragement I continued to receive at home for my pursuit of medicine. Like them, I felt a calling, and when I began school in Shaker Heights that fall, I was more certain than ever that medical research would be a key part of my life's work.

As we settled into our new home, I continued my exploratory wanderings after school, this time in the research labs at nearby Case Western Reserve University. I also hung out at their medical library. The librarian took me aside one day and showed me how to use the *Index Medicus.* In it I could find virtually everything published on any medical subject; I spent weeks poring over it.

For some reason, I became fixated on leukemia, and I started reading everything I could get my hands on about it. I then wrote up my own proposal for a leukemia research project, and brought it to one of the university's staff oncologists. When I dropped off the paper, he smiled patronizingly, as if to say, "Who is this eighth grader?"

It was not terribly original, but it got me into a Case Western apprenticeship program for minority students interested in medicine. The program proved a disappointment, however, because we weren't allowed to do any actual research. After my experience at the University of Pennsylvania, I wasn't interested in listening to people talk; I wanted to work, hands-on, in a research lab.

I finally got my wish at the end of my freshman year in high school, when Dr. Esque Crawford, a well-known obstetrician and a friend of the family, introduced me to Dr. Frederick Cross. Cross was a prominent heart surgeon at Cleveland's St. Luke's Hospital, and coinventor of the Cross-Jones artificial heart valve. "Go talk to my associate, Richard Jones, who runs my lab," Dr. Cross said. That introduction set me on the path to my first scientific discovery.

Although the two men were research colleagues, they were very much a study in personal contrasts. Dr. Cross was your typical impeccably tailored heart surgeon; Dr. Jones, a PhD but not an MD, was a tall, crusty good old boy from the South who chain-smoked Marlboro cigarettes. At the time, their lab was doing heart valve replacement experiments on dogs, as well as canine heart and kidney transplants. "You can work here for the summer," Dr. Jones offered as he puffed away on his Marlboro, "but just as a tech." It was an unpaid position, but that didn't matter to me—I was in the lab at last.

My first assignments were almost janitorial—washing lab glassware and tidying up. Soon, however, Dr. Jones let me draw blood, start IVs, and do other prep work for the surgeries on the dogs. Rapidly thereafter, because I had good technical skills, I was "promoted" to first assistant in surgery—tying knots, sewing, and making incisions. My father and mother would come home and find me practicing my knots and sutures on the family sofa.

Before long, Dr. Jones allowed me to perform entire surgeries. By the tenth grade, I was doing heart valve replacements in dogs, which is a very technical operation, and the dogs would survive. I was even doing some heart transplants. It was a great feeling watching the dogs running around the lab only days after surgery. At the same time, I was also taking college classes—advanced calculus at John Carroll University, and German at Cleveland State University. School always came easy for me.

Eventually, however, I became a bit restless. I wanted to do more. Surgery was challenging, but it was not enough. I didn't want to be just a technician—even a high-level technician—working on someone else's experiments; it was medical discovery that fascinated me. I went to see Dr. Jones in his cubbyhole of an office. "I have a project I'd like to do," I told him.

Artificial heart valves have become increasingly sophisticated over the decades, but at the time, the Cross-Jones valve was very crude. It was basically a cylindrical metal cage with a hard plastic valve that went up and down within it, and I strongly suspected that it had to be damaging red blood cells. My hypothesis was that I would find that the blood cells would be cut, abraded, or mangled when they became trapped between the valve and the cage. These damaged cells would then lose their ability to carry oxygen.

The lab had just purchased one of the first scanning electron microscopes, which produced incredible 3-D images by coating cells with tiny gold particles. I asked Dr. Jones whether I could take blood from the dogs who had received artificial heart valves and then examine their red blood cells under the scanning electron microscope.

"You want to what?" he asked incredulously. He sounded

as if I'd just asked to borrow the brand-new Mercedes for the senior prom, which wasn't far off the mark.

I was asking him to entrust a state-of-the-art $200,000 scanning electron microscope to a teenager. Even though he now had enough confidence in me to let me perform surgery on dogs, Dr. Jones was reluctant at first. Nevertheless, I was very precise and deliberate in explaining the study I was proposing. Moreover, I was able to describe how my methodology would help improve the design of the heart valve that he and Cross had invented. "Okay, go ahead," he finally said.

Before I began my dog blood study, I decided it would be prudent to practice by analyzing human blood. Practice was essential because preparing cells for the scanning electron microscope was a rigorous procedure, and I knew it was important in any research project to follow proper protocol. I had been granted a big opportunity, and I needed to perfect my technique calibrating and using the new equipment.

I had already figured out how I was going to obtain the "practice blood" I needed: One of my fringe benefits was that I was permitted to observe as Dr. Cross performed human open-heart surgery. Without endangering the patient, the anesthesiologist could draw a small quantity of blood for me from the heart-lung bypass machine, after which I'd take it back to the lab and get the red blood cells ready for the scanning electron microscope.

Preparation was a marathon process that took eight

hours to complete. I had to dry the cells; I had to color them with gold particles. Finishing it in one shift would run over into my afternoon class time at Shaker Heights High. Because I couldn't do it all in one day, I would do as much as I could, then incubate the cells overnight at 37 degrees centigrade (body temperature), and finish the following day.

The next morning, however, when I peered at the incubated cells under the scanning electron microscope, I was astonished to see that not all of the red blood cells looked the same. Some appeared deformed. Healthy red blood cells, or discocytes, look like lifesavers—round, but slightly flattened and depressed in the center. What I was seeing under the scope looked like little porcupines. These damaged cells are called echinocytes.

After observing this under the microscope, I incubated some normal blood from volunteers, blood that had not gone through the heart-lung bypass machine. Next day, they were still lifesavers. Since these red blood cells did not appear damaged, I was able to conclude that the heart-lung bypass machine was causing the abnormality.

This was my first encounter with a research phenomenon that might be described as the "odd observation." The outcome may not have been at all what you expected, or even what you had set out to study, but that was precisely what made it so important. In this case, what had started out as a project looking for damage to canine red blood cells from artificial heart valves revealed deformity in human red blood cells from heart bypass machines. While the blood was in the bypass machine, it was getting damaged as it was pumped through rubber tubing in the equipment, but the deformity could only be seen when the cells were incubated at body temperature overnight.

Why did this matter? Because the diameter of a normal red blood cell is about 7–8 microns. A capillary can be just 5 microns, which means that the red blood cells are too big to fit—unless they are able to flex, twist, contort, and squeeze down, like a rubber gasket or a folded parachute, so they can get through. The discoid shape of normal red blood cells allows them to do that. The echinocytes cannot do that. Because of their quills, or spicules, they can't squeeze down small enough. Instead, they get stuck in the capillaries.

The damage to the red blood cells from the heart-lung bypass machine had important medical implications. When echinocytes get clogged in the capillaries, particularly in the brain, they can set off mini-strokes. This was a very plausible explanation why people often end up with memory difficulties and cognitive problems after heart-lung bypass surgery.

When I showed my findings to Dr. Jones, he became very excited. With his encouragement I went back and developed a mathematical formula to describe what I had observed. The discocyte/echinocyte transformation in patients undergoing heart-lung bypass became the subject of my first scientific paper, which I wrote at the age of seventeen. It was published in the *Ohio Journal of Science* when I was a senior at Shaker Heights.

The project won me a Westinghouse Science Award that year, and also helped earn me a spot in what was known as the Interflex program at the University of Michigan School of Medicine. The program no longer exists, but it was designed to get highly motivated aspiring doctors through both an undergraduate degree and an MD in six years, two years ahead of schedule.

Although Interflex was initiated as a way of turning out more compassionate physicians who wanted to be family practitioners, the program drew the best of the best—kids who were in a hurry to become doctors. This was Top Gun for med students. There were only fifty of us in my freshman class, and I was extremely impressed by my fellow "Flexes," with their academic achievements, stellar SATs, and photographic memories.

As I entered the program, I suppose I was leaning toward a career in heart surgery and heart research, especially after all my work in high school with Drs. Cross and Jones. I had to admit, however, that the heart really wasn't that fascinating to me. Then I took my first neuroanatomy class, and I was hooked.

With all due respect for my colleagues in cardiology, the bottom line is that the heart is just a muscle, a pump. To be sure, it's a very elegant muscle and a great pump, but it's still a pump. The brain, on the other hand, is the ultimate reduction of self. We've always romanticized the idea that it's the heart that is the seat of the soul, but surgically we can replace your heart with someone else's heart, and the person who comes out of the OR will still be you. The brain is the one part of the body we cannot damage, cut out, or replace and still be ourselves.

No one wants to die, but the fear of dying of a brain tumor, I would submit, is much greater than the fear of dying of a heart attack. A great deal of the dread isn't the fear of death itself, but the terror of what will happen to you beforehand. As is the case with Alzheimer's disease, if you have a brain tumor that eats away the very essence of who you are, takes away your ability to write, takes away your ability to read, takes away your ability to recognize your loved ones, to speak, to see, to touch, to feel, to move, to have independent thought, takes away your memory—and your memories . . . to me that is far more terrifying. When you lose that, you lose part of the essence of what life is.

I believe this to be something very essential about the human brain. It represents who we are. It represents our personalities, and to a considerable degree it represents what people mean when they talk about the essence of the spirit and the soul. When I discuss fear of surgery with my patients, it's almost never the fear of dying on the table, but the fear of coming out not yourself. No one wants the lamentable fate of Phineas Gage.

Phineas Gage was a nineteenth-century Vermont railway worker. On September 13, 1848, he was laying track when an explosion drove a tamping iron used for packing gunpowder through his head. With the blast, the one-inch diameter, three-foot-long rod became in essence a javelin. It pierced his skull below his left cheek, passed through his frontal lobe, exited the top of his skull, and landed almost thirty yards behind him. To the amazement of everyone, Gage recovered from the accident and was able to return to work—but only briefly. His superficial wounds healed, but the injury to his frontal lobe was severe, and caused a dramatic change in his personality. Characterized before his accident as hardworking, well-balanced, and patient, after the accident he became restless, short-tempered, and given to spewing profanities. Friends described him as "no longer Gage." Tragically, his disability was permanent. It made him a social outcast, and his life spiraled downhill—for a time, he was a circus sideshow attraction. Because of Gage, however, we first came to understand that personality resides in the brain's frontal lobes. This breakthrough was a watershed discovery, and the beginning of the modern age of neuroscience.

This is the frontier where the brain and the mind come together, and the Holy Grail in brain research is to understand the interface between the two. How does the three-pound brain, with its billions of nerve cells, convert the chemical and electrical impulses that it registers into thought and emotion?

We know that even when you look at something that is less complex than the human brain—the brain of a dog, for example—we still cannot answer the question. Dogs have emotions because of the organization of their limbic system. They feel fear; they feel rage. They feel sadness. They get happy. Our brains are more complicated than that, but you can go down into very basic brains that are a fraction of the size of our brains, and still have that same kind of circuitry. There's no doubt. The brain is truly amazing.

There is a well-known passage right in the beginning of the Bible (Genesis 1:27): "God created man in his own image." I believe this to be true, and I believe that if you accept this and you want to come to a more complete understanding of what God is, you must study the brain. There is nothing I know of that God has created that is more beautiful, that is more intricate, and that gives us more insight into what God is than the human brain.

If you want to understand an artist, you study his art. I believe that if you want to understand God, you must study Nature, because Nature is God's art. It's what God has created, and the better you understand Nature, the more insight you get into God.

For me, the anatomy and biochemistry of the human brain is God's greatest art. It is quite simply the most beautiful structure in the known universe. The idea that anyone might liken it to oatmeal or Jell-O or cottage cheese, or consider it ugly, gross, or repulsive, is inconceivable to me. Whenever I look at the pathways and intricacies of the human brain, I am looking at God's art. Every time I operate on the brain, it makes me more spiritual.

By the time I finished the six-year program at Michigan, there was little doubt that I would specialize in neurosurgery, but my first tumor surgery really sealed the deal. I was operating with Dr. Sid Farhad during my second year of residency; he was one of the most technically proficient neurosurgeons I've ever known. Our patient had a sizeable metastatic brain tumor in his left dominant hemisphere. It was squarely in his language area, so it affected his ability to speak, and it was large enough that it also shut down his ability to move. He was paralyzed on his right side, and unable to talk or communicate verbally.

As a second-year resident, I knew that I was expected to do spine cases, take out a ruptured disk or a blood clot. When the operation began, I assumed that my job would be to assist Dr. Farhad. After he called for the scope, however, he stood back and motioned me to take the surgeon's position at the head of the table. By this time I had done a great deal of work with rats and dogs, but this was to be my first time working on a tumor in a human brain.

The surgery went extremely well. This was a tumor that was easily distinguishable from normal brain tissue; not all of them are. We were able to tease the tumor away from the eloquent area of the brain, and it came out very easily. The operation was very satisfying from a technical point of view, because I was able to work under the microscope and remove the tumor. That was nothing, however, compared to the satisfaction I got the next morning on rounds. Just eighteen hours after surgery, the man was freely moving both his right arm and his right leg, and was asking out loud for bacon and eggs.

What an absolute joy! This was a level of gratification I could only imagine before. Working with my hands and my brain, I was able to restore this man's language and his ability to move. It was an exhilaration I wanted to feel again and again.

It is an exhilaration I still feel today. My passion is for science, medicine, and healing. I am aware that I have a gift to do these things well, and that with that gift comes obligation. John Kennedy quoted the Bible (Luke 12:48) when he said, "Of those to whom much is given, much is expected." I still have that sense of calling that I had when I was lurking in the hallways at the University of Pennsylvania as a boy, but it's never a burden. I get to do what I love, every single day.

To me, every operation, every trek into Tiger Country, is an Indiana Jones adventure. And like Indy, I know that if I make one misstep; if I do not approach the adventure with my senses on the highest alert—sight, sound, touch, and smell—the tiger will pounce. One mistake in Tiger Country and my patient on the table will likely pay the consequences—perhaps for the rest of his or her life, or even at the cost of his or her life.

Within the brain there are so many places where the tiger can lie in wait. Whenever I operate, I am ever mindful that the tiger is always lurking, waiting to pounce.

My first encounter with the tiger occurred in 1981, during my final year of residency at Michigan. The old graybeards, as we used to call the senior neurosurgeons, used to tell us horror stories about operations where the pressure had gone so high that the brain squirted out of the skull like Silly String, or jet-propelled toothpaste. Such a notion seemed unreal to me; like the haunted house of childhood, I was sure the old guys were just trying to put a scare in us up-and-coming kids.

I didn't believe any of it until the day I saw it happen—and I was the one at the head of the operating table. As chief resident, I was performing an emergency operation on a thirty-eight-year-old man who had woken up with the worst headache in his life. In our examination we had found two aneurysms, which are blood-filled bulges protruding from weakened arterial walls. Like an automobile tire with a bubble running at seventy mph on the freeway, an aneurysm has a much higher potential for rupture, and must be removed with great care. We had also discovered a huge arteriovenous malformation (AVM), which is an abnormal and potentially lethal snarl of blood vessels.

When we started the operation, we knew it was going to be a long and complex surgery, but we progressed in excellent time, at least early on. I had both aneurysms clipped by 9:30 in the morning before I began to dissect the massive AVM. By 1 p.m. I had taken out 90 percent of it, but a big, draining vein was hindering my progress on the remainder. Two hours later, I had removed only 3 percent more.

At that point I considered cutting the vein, and I discussed it with the attending surgeon, who was assisting me with the surgery. I knew this was not standard procedure, because we had been taught to remove the entire AVM before taking the draining vein. The reasoning was simple: As long as any of the AVM still remained, blood would continue to flow into it, but if you cut the vein, the blood would not have any place to go. By severing the draining vein, you would have built a dam, and blood would pool in the AVM until it ruptured and bled.

Creating a cerebral hemorrhage would never be something I would do deliberately, of course, but as those of us in the OR that afternoon talked it over, we convinced ourselves that although we could not see it, there was yet another vein still draining the AVM. Because we were not 100 percent certain, however, I judiciously decided to test our hypothesis by temporarily clipping the draining vein that was impeding the surgery. We then waited to see what effect this would have.

What we were hoping was that nothing would happen. If shutting down the vein had no effect—if the blood flow did not diminish—we could conclude that our initial assessment was correct and that there was indeed another draining vein deep below the AVM, beyond our view. At that point I could confidently cut the draining vein that was in plain sight and then dissect the rest of the AVM.

We waited ten minutes after temporarily clipping the vein. Nothing happened, so I went ahead and cut the vein.

Obviously we had not waited long enough, because as soon as I severed the vessel, the end of the vein stood up like a newly aroused king cobra emerging from a snake charmer's basket. The pressure was so high that the vein, which is usually relaxed, instantly became engorged and erect. That was the first sign that we had a very big problem.

"Indiana Black" had inadvertently sprung the booby trap, and the tiger had pounced. I still had another 7 percent of the AVM to remove, but every time I touched the area it started spurting blood, and it would take us thirty minutes of feverish activity to stop it. We repeatedly packed the area to stop the bleeding, but it would always start all over again as soon as I resumed the dissection.

This went on for three or four hours. Finally under the surgical microscope I saw my own worst nightmare looming before me. My patient's entire brain started swelling, rising up out of his skull, just like bread dough. At that point, Tiger Country looked a lot like the Temple of Doom.

The graybeards had been telling the truth, but I hadn't really believed it until I saw it with my own eyes. It was at about this time that the attending surgeon fell back on the old school way of doing things. He called for the large glass suckers—powerful extractors that are the medical counterpart of the turkey baster. They would surely remove all the blood we had been struggling to control, but like a turkey baster they would suck up not just blood but everything else in their path as well. I'd already heard plenty of frightening and ultimately tragic accounts about the damage they could do to the brain, and I was keenly aware that my patient faced the prospect of grave neurological injury if they were deployed.

I needed to act quickly. I knew we had only one hope—my patient had only one hope—and that was for me to ignore the blood and get rid of that last 7 percent of the arterial venous malformation as fast as I could. It was a desperation gambit, a Hail Mary pass with no time on the clock, as I worked through a pool of rising brain and blood to dissect what was left of the AVM.

All of a sudden, the bleeding stopped. It was astonishing, as if the floodwaters abruptly receded just before the drowning men—in this case my patient and me—went under for the last time. And at that moment, the brain quieted down and settled back into place.

Next morning we were making rounds and my patient looked up to me, his head bandaged, with a cheerful smile on his face. "Thanks, Doc," he said. "You did a really great job." I breathed a huge sigh of relief. It was the best outcome imaginable for a guy I thought was never going to make it off the table. My patient had emerged from his ordeal neurologically intact, and had no clue that he had almost died. No good would come from bringing it up with him now, but I thought for a very long time about the lessons I learned from that surgery. One of those lessons would stay with me for life: The need to plan out every operation in full, and to have a game plan for any eventuality.

What I had not yet fully realized at that early stage in my career was that the medicine and surgery aside, a patient's steely resolve to fight the disease and to persevere in the face of a daunting diagnosis is at least as powerful as any drug or procedure in the physician's arsenal. Science and technology keep giving us new weapons against brain cancer, but the tumor is a formidable adversary, and fighting it is a constant battle. There are risks involved—risks of the highest level: of life and death, pain and disability—and my patients must deal with these on a daily basis. Even when they know that the odds of a complete "cure" are against them, they face these risks with incredible personal courage. The chance for a longer life with loved ones is their cherished reward, which is why when I tell them what the risks are and they choose to fight, I'm ready to go into battle with them—and for them.

CHAPTER 3

Risks and Rewards

Gerard Kelly, age thirty-five, came to Cedars-Sinai Medical Center with a very large brain tumor. He arrived with his younger brother Thomas, and it was something of a miracle that they were here at all. They were of modest means, and came from a small town outside of Dublin, Ireland. They had found me on the Internet after a worldwide search for someone who could treat the clival chordoma, a slow-growing but nevertheless life-threatening tumor that originates out of the clivus bone at the base of the brain, making it particularly difficult to get to. It lies there, growing, like an ogre under a bridge.

It had taken every penny the Kellys could muster, including loans the family took out and contributions from virtually everyone in their village, to get themselves to Los Angeles and to fund the operation. They had also received help from the Irish government, which provides financial assistance for treatment elsewhere when certain kinds of medical services are not available inside the country. Even the forklift company Mr. Kelly had worked for—which had continued to pay his salary during his protracted sick leave—kicked in. The Kellys had come in through the office of International Health Services at Cedars, which had informed them of the costs, collected and forwarded the MRI films to me, and helped the brothers with their travel and lodging arrangements so that my team could evaluate the case. Cedars itself had agreed to underwrite a modest portion of the cost—that is, if we could do the operation at all.

"Are you sure you really want to do this surgery?" Suzane Brian, my physician's assistant, asked me as we examined Mr. Kelly's MRI scans before seeing him in the clinic. It was not an easy question to answer. Gerard Kelly had what was perhaps the largest clival chordoma I'd ever seen. I expected that if we performed surgery, it would have to be done in two phases. He was going to be away from his home base of support for some time, and Suzane was particularly concerned about the advanced stage of his tumor and the logistics of his long-term care.

For my part, I wasn't sure how much I could accomplish in this case, but from the moment I walked into the examining room, my heart had gone out to the two personable, working-class brothers. Even though both men were in their thirties, they still had a homespun boyish innocence about them. I sensed the strong bond between them instantly. Gerard had always been the rock, the center of strength in the Kelly family. Good with his hands, he'd started his own furniture manufacturing company in the late 1990s. He was twenty-five and his company was doing well when he had his first seizure. Irish neurosurgeons had performed two operations. The first was successful, and was followed by a series of radiation treatments, but it took Gerard a couple of years to fully recover. Unable to sustain his furniture business, he nevertheless rebuilt his life, taking a job as a forklift operator and buying his first house. He even managed to put money aside to cover the mortgage if the tumor reappeared, as more than half of all clival chordomas do.

"A few years later Gerard started to get neck pains," Thomas told me. "He was playing football and got a bang in the face with the ball. For a time he tried to chalk it up to that, but then there were other symptoms. He went into denial, I think. Then one day his eye just turned all the way in. We went to the hospital and they told us he had a regrowth of the tumor."

Gerard underwent another surgery; this time it was not successful. The surgeon encountered problems with the extensive regrowth and with the texture of the tumor, which had grown firm and rubbery from the radiation treatments. He backed out after removing only a small portion of it, and declared its remaining bulk inoperable. He then gave Gerard and his family the worst possible news, saying that the young man had only a few months to live. There was nothing more to be done, he said.

If only they had found Cedars sooner, I thought to myself. The second Irish neurosurgeon had approached the tumor through the back of the head, and his means of entry had violated the dura mater, the covering of the brain beneath the skull, and in so doing he had set the ogre loose. No longer sandwiched between the dura and the skull, the unfettered clival chordoma had mushroomed as it grew into the breach. It expanded into the brain, and then coiled itself around the brain stem and all of its surrounding blood vessels. After that it crept down the spine, all the way to the cervical vertebrae at the top of the neck.

As Suzane and I entered the examining room that morning, both young men stood up. Gerard rose with some difficulty, but broad smiles swept across their unmistakably Irish faces. "We can't believe we're actually here," Thomas told me excitedly. "It's like a dream." Gerard Kelly was the fairer skinned and the shorter of the two, dressed simply in a jacket, jeans, a white T-shirt, and red tennis shoes. Thomas Kelly was also dressed in jeans, with a green T-shirt and tennis shoes. He was over six feet tall, but he clearly looked up to his older brother, awed by his persistent courage in the face of his ongoing ordeal, which now spanned almost a decade.

Gerard Kelly looked at me as if I was his last hope. His eyes, I noted, were not tracking well, and he was having trouble maintaining his balance—all due to compression on various nerves and on the brain stem from the tumor.

His hearing had also deteriorated. A permanent feeding tube, which he wore under his shirt, had been implanted into his stomach because he was unable to swallow. "Can you do the surgery?" he managed. Because the tumor was pressing on the nerves servicing his vocal cords, his voice was muffled and his words did not come easily.

I didn't give a direct answer. "Why don't you come with me and we'll look at the films together," I offered, leading the two brothers out of the examining room and into the viewing room next door. A moment later Gerard's tumor was up on the screen, and their charming smiles vanished.

To my surprise, this was the first time that the Kellys had actually beheld their adversary. Their previous neurosurgeons had not gone over the MRI scans with them. Now they could see the tumor for the vast, hydra-headed monster that it was. It was a daunting sight to me as well.

The two brothers were overwhelmed, speechless. "Gerard," Thomas said softly, "that's why the doctors in Ireland gave you only a few months to live."

"Why didn't they show us this before?" Gerard Kelly asked finally. He was clearly annoyed that this information had been withheld from him. "Can you do the operation?" he repeated anxiously.

"It would be a very difficult and very complicated surgery," I began. "On a scale of one to ten, this operation would be a ten-plus. In fact, it would take two operations. There would be serious risks, including stroke, paralysis, and infection."

"Does this mean you won't do it?" Thomas asked.

"No," I said. "The surgery, though very difficult, is possible."

"I know I can't live like this," Gerard replied hoarsely. He was barely audible. "I'm getting worse."

"I'm afraid that the radiation treatments you received made things even more difficult. It created scarring that will be hard to deal with. I can't guarantee you that I will be able to get all of the tumor out, but at the very least I think I will be able to buy you some additional time."

There was a look of grim but unwavering determination on Gerard's face. "I want to go forward," he said without hesitation. "Whatever the outcome, I'm prepared." Thomas Kelly nodded in agreement. They had been weighing their alternatives for some time. They understood the risks of surgery, but they believed the potential rewards were worth it.

That was exactly the attitude I needed to see. When patients choose to have surgery, some may wonder whether they're doing the right thing. Not the Kellys. In poker terms, the brothers were all in. "Okay, then," I said. "We'll move forward together."

While Gerard Kelly's surgery would be difficult, it would be nothing like those performed by pioneering physician Harvey Cushing in the early 1900s. Back then, brain surgery was almost as deadly as the brain tumors themselves. At first it was very often fatal. Cushing, the first modern neurosurgeon to operate in Tiger Country, went in without the drugs and equipment we consider essential today, because they had not yet been developed. He had no surgical microscope, no steroids to control brain swelling, and no antibiotics. Of necessity, his technique was crude: He used his finger to literally scoop the tumor out of the brain.

It took a great deal of courage to do what he did; many of his patients died in surgery, and almost all who survived emerged with life-altering deficits. Nevertheless, Cushing was able to offer a glimmer of hope to those who had none whatsoever, and his empathy with his patients was legendary. By the 1920s he was performing 300 operations a year, and making improvements in technique and survivorship as he went along. Cushing is considered the father of modern neurosurgery. He trained virtually the entire generation of neurosurgeons that followed him. For the next half century, improvements in neurosurgery came in fits and starts.

My student days at the University of Michigan in the late 1970s were the beginning of a heady time of progress in neuroscience. Technological advances were providing doctors with more analytical weapons than ever before. New brain imaging tools such as computerized tomography (CT), positron emission tomography (PET), and magnetic resonance imaging (MRI) gave us the ability to see more of the brain, from more angles, in greater detail, than ever before—without exploratory surgery. It was also the dawn of the computer age, and it wasn't long before the two emerging fields began to mesh. The discoveries, however, were not always speedily deployed in the operating room. Even when I finished my residency in the late 1980s, patients with large tumors who came out of surgery were very sick. They would spend days in the ICU; they would have significant neurological deficits.

Today that is no longer acceptable. Not only do my patients survive surgery, but most survive without deficits and go home in a matter of days. In fact, most of what I learned in my residency has become obsolete. The surgical techniques I'm using now are not the techniques we used then; twenty years from now I hope to be able to say the same thing about what we do today. Neurosurgery is constantly evolving, and advances in the field are moving faster than ever. If you don't keep up through conferences and the literature, it's easy to become a dinosaur.

Until recent years, metastatic brain tumors weren't considered worth treating aggressively via surgery. There are two types of tumors: primary and metastatic. A primary originates in the brain. A metastatic starts somewhere else. Of these two types, metastatic tumors are far more common. If current trends continue, there will be about 22,000 new cases of primary brain tumors in the United States in 2008, and 170,000 brain metastases. The thinking was that these tumors could not be controlled, and that the surgical risks were too high. Time and experience, however, has progressed past this thinking, and one of my patients is living proof.

I first saw Scott Erdman in 1991, when I was still on the neurosurgery staff at UCLA Medical Center. I couldn't help but notice that he and I were almost exactly the same age. By the time I saw him in my office at UCLA, he had already survived multiple bouts with malignant melanoma.

The first had been discovered a decade earlier. "It was 1981 when my fiancée Pam, now my wife, and I were watching a tennis match on TV. I was leaning back, putting my hands behind my head," Scott remembers. "She reached over to give me a hug and felt a bump in my armpit. Just a bump, but a week later it was still there. One member of our church congregation was an oncologist, and he took a look at it. Odds were about 99 to 1 that it was an inflamed lymph node, he told me, but he said I should go to UCLA for a biopsy, just in case.

"They found melanoma and performed radical surgery to treat it. They removed a tumor and twenty-four surrounding lymph nodes, thirteen of which were infiltrated with cancerous melanoma cells. In 1986 I was a divinity student at Fuller Theological Seminary in Pasadena. Pam and I had a small celebration to mark my five-year cancer-free anniversary, but our party was premature. Just one month later, they found it had spread to my gut. The surgeons at UCLA removed a malignant melanoma and about eight inches of my small intestine. Two years later, they removed yet another one."

By 1991 Scott was a young pastor at Bel Air Presbyterian Church, and he had started having severe headaches.

An MRI scan revealed three metastatic melanoma tumors in his brain. The largest was the size of an orange in his right frontal lobe, the brain's CEO. The two others were smaller, but were likewise located in highly sensitive areas of the brain. One was in the parietal lobe, which enables us to find our way around in the world. Some language function is located there as well. The other was in the temporal lobe, which enables us to interpret smells and sounds, and also contributes to visual and verbal memory.

At that time, surgery to remove multiple metastatic tumors in the brain was not the officially sanctioned course of treatment. In fact, it was not recommended at all. Neurosurgeons were concerned not only about the high incidence of post-surgical deficits, but also about their inability to get all of the tumor out. As a result, patients would end up with all the deficits and no increased longevity. The failure to achieve an image-complete resection, coupled with the likelihood of neurological damage from the operation, tilted the risk-benefit ratio into the negative. Surgery, it was said, would only cause the dying additional pain and suffering.

UCLA's radiation oncologist, who was also consulting with me on Scott's case, subscribed to this point of view, and was adamant about treating him exclusively with whole brain radiation. "Surgery is too dangerous; many people die after that," he declared. "Radiation to his entire brain will buy him six months—and that is the best we can do."

I didn't believe that for a moment, and said so. The

oncologist was adamantly holding out for whole brain radiation. I argued that going ahead with surgery to get the tumor out was a better course of action. "We need to do something more radical," I insisted.

If we stuck with whole brain radiation, we all knew going in that Scott would have only enough time to put his affairs in order and say farewell to his loved ones. In my mind, I could see no reason not to give him at least a chance of surviving longer than six months. Although at the time my approach was outside the bounds of the standard of care, I felt that pushing the envelope had a greater chance of success. I thought I could do better; I surely didn't think I could do any worse.

Was it worth having an open dispute with a colleague in front of a patient, something I would ordinarily make every effort to avoid? Most doctors would have given Scott the whole brain radiation and called it a day. To me that was not good enough, and I felt strongly that I had a responsibility to speak up. Oddly enough, I had the same issues with whole brain radiation that the oncologist had with surgery: I didn't think it was going to work, and I knew it had great potential to create serious collateral damage. You can't really crank up the amount of whole brain radiation high enough to destroy the tumor without destroying a lot of healthy brain tissue; it's akin to swatting at fleas in a bearskin rug with a hatchet. And with melanoma it would be even less useful, because melanoma tumors tend to be radiation-resistant.

Further defying the conventional wisdom, I believed I had a good shot at controlling the tumors in his brain with surgery. I was in fact quite optimistic, because thanks to his previous operations, at the time Scott had no evidence of tumor growth elsewhere in his body. When a metastatic tumor comes to the brain, it's critical to know how well the disease is controlled elsewhere. If the disease is all over the body, there's no point in treating the brain tumor.

Scott had no sign of active melanoma outside the brain, so I felt I could be very aggressive in treating his tumors. Moreover, the largest of them was in an area of the frontal lobe that was clear of his language and motor areas, giving me an excellent chance to achieve an image-complete resection with very low risk of post-surgical deficits. Once this tumor was surgically removed, I figured we could deliver a knockout blow to the smaller temporal and parietal tumors with stereotactic radiation therapy, also known as the XKnife, which was new at the time.

The XKnife is a noninvasive surgical tool that directs focused X-ray beams into the brain from a ring around the patient's skull. The equipment is a bit like a big dental X-ray machine that rotates around the head. Unlike whole brain radiation, these X-rays can be aimed specifically at the tumor, guided by an MRI scanner and a computer. Where the beams intersect, the dose of radiation is high enough to destroy all of the cancer cells, with minimal damage to surrounding healthy brain. The procedure is akin to burning a piece of paper with a magnifying glass, and had already shown great promise in dealing with metastatic tumors.

I was fairly certain that with surgery and the XKnife, I could give Scott as much as an extra year and a half, perhaps more, but because there was not a consensus between the oncologist and me, Scott had to make the call himself. Although the oncologist had to be reminded that the patient was entitled to cast the tiebreaker, Scott didn't hesitate. "I want a chance for a longer survival," the young pastor told us definitively. "Give me surgery and the XKnife."

Was Scott's surgery going to be worth it? I had little doubt that it would be. Barring any serious complications—and these had already become rare—I knew that I was going to extend his life span, and that it would be time well spent.

The surgery on Scott's largest tumor went very smoothly. Actual excision of the tumor took just an hour, and he was in and out of the OR in about four hours, with no post-surgical deficits. I was particularly impressed with how well the XKnife subsequently worked on his two smaller tumors.

This was not the end of his treatment, however. The following year, 1992, I found another tumor, this time on his right temporal lobe. I performed a second craniotomy to remove it. In 1995 I treated a small, suspicious area I saw on his MRI scan with focused radio waves, using a new needle-like probe we developed for metastatic brain tumors. The suspicious area on the MRI, however, turned out not to be a tumor after all.

Today I still get a big smile every time I see Scott Erdman. Seventeen years after his first brain tumor surgery, he is very much alive; he is a remarkable survivor. Now a pastor at Hollywood Presbyterian Church, he comes in annually for a follow-up MRI scan; for many years now he's been tumor-free.

Without our aggressive treatment, he wouldn't have had a chance, but I give a great deal of credit for his survival to his strong faith and equally strong network of support. I have always found a patient's faith and strong support from friends and family to be the greatest allies. It's not adherence to any particular religion, but rather a belief in a spiritual life that goes beyond what we can see. Is this God at work? Or is this the power of the mind working to cure the body? Perhaps it's a combination.

As I've said, people with brain tumors are grateful for any extra days or months you can give them. If I can give them another six months or year of quality life, I'll do it.

Always.

I see a lot of patients like Scott Erdman and Gerard Kelly, who have come in after other doctors have "given up" on them. "You have a brain tumor," they've been told. "There's not a lot we can do, so there's no point in us really trying to give you optimal treatment." To me that's the entirely wrong attitude to take. I didn't take it with Scott Erdman, and I didn't take it with Gerard Kelly.

Twenty years ago Gerard Kelly's clival chordoma was considered inoperable, and the diagnosis was a death sentence. Getting to the tumor was always the problem. Early on, some neurosurgeons did attempt heroic efforts to remove clival chordomas by going in through the brain for the resection. Their patients—those who actually survived the procedure itself—most often came out comatose, awaiting death. Left untreated, however, the clival chordoma would eventually compress the brain stem, with the same result.

It took the development of a novel surgical approach to make these tumors accessible. Called skull base surgery, the new technique attacked the tumor by going in via the nose or mouth, rather than through the brain. I participated with a broad interdisciplinary team of neurosurgeons, head and neck surgeons, and oral, plastic, and orbital surgeons to develop it. The procedure had actually been first described in 1929 by an ear, nose, and throat surgeon, who did not dare venture into the brain. It was lost until we resurrected it and brought modern technology to bear. Nevertheless, skull base surgery is challenging. It is difficult to perform, and tougher on the patient than most brain surgeries, but patients with this deeply invasive tumor can now be treated. The clival chordoma has gone from being a deadly tumor to being a curable tumor, in the right hands.

Gerard Kelly never asked me if he was going to die. Because of the tumor's extensive growth in and around the structures at the base of his brain and down his spine, we all knew that the odds of an outright cure were against him. The risks were real, but the benefits were too. Gerard and his brother were firmly committed, and because they were committed, I was as well. I intended to do everything I could, within the realm of acceptable risk, to give this brave young man his best chance for a longer life.

Gerard was visibly relieved when I told him he would get his operation at last. I could see the tension drain from his body. "Do it as quickly as you can," he pleaded, giving me a thumbs-up and the best smile he could muster.

I nodded and looked at Suzane. "We'll set the first surgery up for Thursday." That was much easier said than done. She would have to round up all the members of the interdisciplinary surgical team and orchestrate our schedules to book the procedure.

"Am I going to be in a lot of pain?" Gerard asked.

"No," I assured him. "We'll be able to keep you comfortable with medications."

The goal of the first surgery was to set the stage for the second. In it we would seek to achieve a degree of separation between the tumor, the brain stem, and the surrounding structures. When the chordoma had grown into the subarachnoid space, the fluid-filled area between the dura and the brain, it had wrapped itself around his vertebral and basilar arteries—the major arteries supplying blood to the brain stem. Any damage to either of these arteries would result in a massive brain-stem stroke. In addition, the membrane that separated the tumor from Mr. Kelly's brain stem appeared to have been obliterated, resulting in swelling and inflammation in both his brain stem and the spinal cord.

To achieve our objective, I entered through the side and back of the skull, where it attaches to the spinal column surrounding the spinal cord. This is called a far lateral skull base approach, and it was going to allow me enough access to isolate the vertebral artery and separate it from the tumor. Beginning below the area where the tumor had started to invade the spinal cord and the brain stem, I very carefully dissected it away under the operating microscope. It was a delicate process, but I accomplished what I set out to do. I was able to achieve a significant decompression of the brain stem, and also managed to remove about 30 percent of the clival chordoma itself.

Gerard Kelly rebounded well from this first operation. A day after surgery he was up and walking, and his symptoms were noticeably improved. The operation improved his hearing and his ability to swallow, and also gave him a bit more stamina. He was able to sit up in a chair longer without fatigue. We still had a long and precarious way to go, but I could see the hope rekindle in Gerard's eyes. The biggest smile in the room, however, belonged to Thomas, who was beaming at his brother's marked improvement so soon after surgery.

The bigger and more grueling task—getting the remaining 70 percent of the tumor—was still to come, and nearly all of it was right in the heart of Tiger Country. Having just been in the neighborhood, I realized that this second surgery would be as tough as they get. It would take everything I had and then some to avoid coming face-to-face with the tiger.

It was several weeks after the first operation and right after Thanksgiving when we took on the second phase of Gerard's surgery. I stepped up to the operating table at 1:00 p.m., but the procedure had started several hours earlier. My colleagues Geno Hunt, a neurosurgeon, and Jeffrey Hammoudeh, a plastic surgeon/otolaryngologist, had performed the opening and had exposed the tumor for me, which in this case was no small task. Previously I had accessed the tumor by entering through the side and back of Gerard's skull; now we were going right in the front door, through Gerard's mouth and nose. It took Geno and Jeff three hours to create a passageway to the tumor through the sinuses and the hard palate.

This is called an anterior skull base approach. If a clival chordoma lies entirely above the hard palate, you can usually get at it by going through the nose. If it is sitting below the hard palate, you can access it by entering through the mouth. In Gerard's case, however, the tumor had grown both above and below the hard palate, so we had to do both. The doctors performed what is called a LaForte osteotomy, splitting his hard palate and his upper jawbone right down the middle. This allowed us to access everything from the skull base to the pituitary gland, but it still was not enough. The tumor had grown down Gerard's spinal column, all the way to the third cervical vertebra, which is in the upper part of the neck.

The only way to get to this part of the chordoma was to split Gerard's tongue and lower jaw in half, as we had done with the hard palate and upper jawbone. In essence, we split his face entirely open below the nose and swung everything—jawbone, hard palate, teeth, and tongue—out to either side.

To those outside the medical community, this hugely invasive surgery sounds shocking, even grotesque, but it was nothing more than the monster required. This is why I had been looking for Gerard's game face before I agreed to take the case, and why his staunch commitment and resolve were so crucial. When he consented to surgery, I had to be sure he knew what was in store for him.

The opening procedure also involved a tracheotomy, because otherwise the breathing tube would have been in the surgical field, blocking access to the tumor. Splitting the jaw had to be flawless, and the two surgeons expertly placed screws and plates in the maxilla and mandible before dividing them, so that everything would fit back together perfectly. If the reconstruction was so much as a millimeter off, Gerard Kelly would face a life of pain and would never be able to eat normally again. With their skill and experience, our surgeons were able to accomplish this without cutting up Gerard's face. Geno and Jeff went in under the lip so they would not leave him disfigured. Unfortunately, this had not been the case with his first surgery in Ireland, and Gerard still bore a prominent scar alongside his nose and down to the center of his upper lip.

With everything exposed from the pituitary down to the cervical spine, the path was finally clear for me to dissect out the clival chordoma under the surgical microscope. "Okay, let's get the scope in," I said at 1:05 p.m. The lights came down in the OR as the dissecting microscope was maneuvered into place and the surgical beams focusing on the tumor were turned on.

"Let's keep an eye on the blood loss," I cautioned to Bob Naruse, the anesthesiologist. "Has anybody ordered more blood?"

"This is the only other unit we have right now, Dr. Black," he replied. "I've ordered more, but it's not here yet."

This was an issue of concern. In the process of splitting his face and exposing the tumor, Gerard had lost a considerable amount of blood. When I entered the OR, we were already a little below optimal in our blood supply. If I hit a blood vessel—and I was going to be working around the carotid artery—we could lose a lot more blood very rapidly. If we didn't have enough on hand, Gerard could go into cardiac arrest on the table.

I started by making sure I had good exposure above and

below the tumor and off to each side. By 1:50, that task had been accomplished. I could now begin the dissection, starting at the top and working my way down, cutting and peeling the tumor away from the surrounding structures, using the micro dissectors, which look like miniature chopsticks, and micro scissors. In all, we were looking at what could become a ten-to-twelve-hour surgery, of which my part would be about half. We had no guarantee that we could get it all out, but the risk-benefit ratio was still tilting positive. Twenty years earlier, there was no way we would have gotten even this far.

Nobody uttered a word. All of us in the OR were wearing our own game faces now. Everyone was intently focused on the surgery and in perfect synch with one another. And in terms of the surgery we were looking good, at least so far. Unlike many other tumors, a clival chordoma has a very distinctive appearance, and I had defined the borders of the gray, gelatinous tumor mass from the pituitary gland all the way to the brain stem, and then down the spinal column to C3—the third cervical vertebra. The surgical path was clear.

"We're in no-man's-land," I announced as I looked at the ogre before me. Millimeter by millimeter, my hands steady and my mind focused on the dissection, I stripped the tumor away. Eventually we came to the bottom of the clivus—the bone at the base of the skull where the tumor had originated. Because the tumor had embedded itself in the spine, I would also have to bore out the compromised bone from the vertebrae. Using a high-speed diamond burr drill, I drilled out the clivus, the anterior part of the first spinal arch, and the front part of the second.

"Blood loss is up to one thousand," Dr. Naruse said. "He's got two units of blood now and we've got two more units on the way."

"Okay," I replied.

I was eventually able to liberate all of Gerard's spinal cord. I managed to remove 95 percent of the tumor and was down to the last bit on the brain stem, but that was where I ran into a roadblock. The problem was scarring. Because of his radiation treatments and the prior surgeries, everything in the lower part of the brain stem was scarred in. The last 5 percent of the tumor was adhering tenaciously to the medulla, which is the lower part of the brain stem, and to the surrounding vessels. The vertebral arteries run just in front of the medulla oblongata. Nearby are the nerves that control swallowing, facial movement, and other functions. I could not see how I could peel off the tumor without affecting these crucial structures.

I worked on it for a while with the micro dissectors, attempting to develop even the smallest plane that would permit me to separate the tumor from the brain stem. I was trying to locate that one dividing cell layer that would allow me to peel the tumor away, but it just wasn't there. The only way to get the last of the tumor—which was now down to the size of half a pencil eraser—would carry with it a great risk of neurological damage.

Here in the heart of Tiger Country, the risk-benefit seesaw went negative. There was no way I was going to chance giving Gerard Kelly a brain-stem stroke and induce a coma. I knew the clival chordoma would grow back, but if it grew back away from the brain stem rather than toward it, I'd bought him another three or four years. At that point, I would perhaps be able to do another surgery. If it grew into the brain stem, however, there would be nothing more I could do.

I stepped back to allow Drs. Hunt and Hammoudeh to begin the critical lengthy closing procedure. I left the operating room, physically spent and mentally drained from the battle. I had met the Tiger head-on and come out with a measure of victory. It wasn't everything we'd hoped for, but Gerard Kelly had gotten his gift of time.

A week later, some twenty days before Christmas, I would perform a third surgery on Gerard to stabilize his spine. Since the tumor had invaded the front part of the spinal column, I had bored out a significant amount of bone. As a result, his skull was no longer firmly anchored in position. Like a golf ball sitting on a tee, it was possible for his head to literally fall off the vertebral column. If it did so, there was a danger that it would pinch the spinal cord, causing instant paralysis. In a two-hour operation, we installed screws and plates to keep his head in alignment and reattach it to the spine. During this follow-up procedure, I was also able to remove a bit more of the tumor, so that 98 percent of the clival chordoma was now gone.

Gerard's fourth and last operation was a procedure to close a tiny spinal fluid leak. Because of the radiation he had received in Ireland, one of my biggest concerns from the outset was that his tissues would not heal well in the area that had been radiated. Once we breached the barrier between the mouth and the spinal fluid, bacteria from the mouth and the nose could go right into the brain, causing life-threatening meningitis. As a cautionary measure, he had been placed on antibiotics before surgery, and several days after the operation I took him back into the OR and repacked the area with fat and fascia to get a watertight seal.

Gerard faced a long and complex recovery. The tracheal tube we had inserted so that he could breathe during surgery would remain in place for weeks, until the swelling went down and he was able to breathe through his nose again. He would also be wearing a neck brace for some time until the spine stabilization had healed.

By this time the Cedars-Sinai volunteers were starting to prepare for the holidays, and it was beginning to look a lot like Christmas on the floor. Gerard Kelly had been through as much heavy-duty surgery as almost any patient I could remember, but at first he was happy to be alive, and happy to hear that we had been able to remove so much of his tumor. To a great degree, we were able to control his pain through medication, but his face was badly swollen, his jaw was wired shut, his neck brace immobilized him, and of course he still had the breathing tube and the feeding tube. As a result, he could not speak. A pad and pencil by his bedside was now the only communication lifeline between the two brothers.

Initially, his spirits were good, but about a week after his surgery, Gerard Kelly began to slide into a deep depression. I knew if I could just get him through the next few weeks of recovery, he would start to be himself again, buoyed by the promise of years of good life with his brother and his family. Each day as I visited him and monitored his healing, however, I saw that he was becoming more remote. I feared that he was losing his will to live.

Ten days after his big operation, Suzane came to me in tears. On the pad Gerard kept by his bedside, she saw the words he had written to Thomas earlier that day: "Please bring me a gun so I can end all of this."

A few moments later, I stood by his bedside. Suzane had been right to be upset. He looked like a young man who had been in a terrible fight and lost—and not because of his dramatic bruising and all the tubes and braces. The deadened look in his eyes was the look of a man who had given up. Thomas Kelly sat nearby, his eyes swollen with tears. I had been continually impressed with Thomas's dedication to his brother. He spent all day, every day, with Gerard, telling stories and keeping his spirits up.

"Gerard, you're going to be okay," I said, trying to reassure him.

There was no reply. His hand didn't stir to reach for his pencil. His face, swollen and distorted, betrayed no expression. "Look," I said, "I know you're in pain and things seem bad now, but you're going to feel a lot better soon, and then you'll be going home. I promise you."

Again, no response. The breathing tube was doing its job, but all it was doing was keeping him alive. Thomas told me what had happened when Gerard woke up in the ICU, after I had repaired the spinal fluid leak. "He was lying on the bed," he recalled, "and he thought he was dead. He was wondering why everybody else was in the room. At that stage he wanted to be gone."

I had seen patients in this state before, but only rarely, because the recovery period after brain surgery is usually pretty quick. Despite all the meds we were giving him, Gerard Kelly was still in pain. And his suffering went deeper, beyond the reach of anesthetics. Calling to him that day was like calling down a tunnel, and yet somehow I knew he was still there.

"Is there anything I can get you?" I asked.

No reply.

"C'mon, Gerard," Thomas coaxed. "You're going to get better. We're going to buy Christmas gifts for the nephews back in Ireland. You'll be playing with them again soon, like you love to do. You'll see. Everything is going to be fine."

I thought for a moment, and then I made what was a deliberately outrageous proposal. "Gerard, how 'bout I go out and get some whiskey, and we can have a drink together?" It would be a while before he would be able to drink it, of course, but the idea struck me as a good one.

That turned out to be the offer he couldn't refuse. A smile crept across the young man's swollen face, and the light came back in his eyes. Then he raised his hand slowly and gave me his signature thumbs-up—the same gesture he had given me when we first discussed his surgery. Gerard Kelly was back. Behind me, I could hear Thomas crying.

A few moments later, Mr. Kelly picked up his pad and wrote, "Will I be home for Christmas?"

"No," I said, "but you'll be home for *next* Christmas."

His smile got broader still.

"You Irish have it right," I said. "Faith and whiskey, and you'll get through."

With a little help from your friends.

After that day, Suzane Brian became a woman on a mission. If Gerard Kelly could not go home for Christmas, she would bring Christmas to Gerard Kelly. Suzane is particularly sensitive to international patients. She and her family had been forced to flee her native Peru after Shining Path guerrillas attempted to assassinate her physician father. They left so quickly that there was no time to say good-bye or to grab precious photos. She knew all too well how difficult it is to be far from home, separated from family and comforting surroundings, especially at the holidays. After Thomas told her that Gerard had always loved Christmas, Suzane went shopping for little Christmas trees and decorations. She fomented a delightful and merry conspiracy among the nursing staff, resulting in a shower of little gifts and surprises for our patient.

Gerard was particularly delighted by one of Suzane's special purchases, a pair of spiffy designer pajamas from Bloomingdale's, wrapped up in the biggest bow imaginable. On Christmas morning the staff helped Gerard into his new pj's so he could celebrate the holiday with his brother. A young woman from the Cedars-Sinai volunteer service played Christmas carols on the violin. When Thomas arrived, Gerard was beaming, but the biggest gift of all could not be gift-wrapped. Thomas was not alone. As a surprise, their sister had flown in from Ireland to be with Gerard. At one point, Mr. Kelly picked up his pad and pencil and wrote, "I just wish I could have my voice back to be able to say thank you."

That was the turning point in his convalescence. Once again, faith, friends, and family—however you want to define any of them—had made a huge difference in the recovery of one of my patients. And the whiskey? The little bottles I had bought for Gerard sat in a place of honor on the shelf near the bed. "We're not going to drink them," Thomas Kelly said with a smile. "We're going to get them framed."

Before long, the two brothers were walking the corridors together, arm in arm. Gerard was leaning on his younger brother, who had insisted that he no longer use the walker. Several weeks after the turn of the new year, they flew home to Ireland. Just before their departure, Thomas Kelly received a text message from his brother-in-law saying, "We are looking forward to your arrival on Saturday. With all the preparations, it's like the Papal visit."

That following March, Thomas Kelly called from his mother's house in Ireland, where Gerard was staying, to tell us that although his tongue was still a bit swollen, his brother was recuperating nicely. I was not surprised; I had just received his latest MRI films from his Irish doctor, and they looked very good indeed.

Although some might find the surgery to have been drastic, Thomas was at peace with the decision. "We prayed for a miracle and we got one," he said. "Not many people get them, you know? Gerard has so much heart. If he needed surgery tomorrow, I'd find a way. I'd do it all over again."

In the background I could hear Gerard Kelly laughing, playing with his nephews.

CHAPTER 4

Thoughtful Warriors in the Brain

People often ask me if I ever get nervous during surgery. The answer is no. If I see people who are nervous in the operating room, it makes *me* nervous. Why? Because it indicates to me that in all likelihood they are unsure of what they are doing.

Working within the brain is very complicated, highly technical, highly precise surgery, with a high degree of risk, which means I do not want to see any brain surgeons in the OR who appear jittery or uncertain. If they look worried going into the operating room, chances are they are not well-prepared, not well-planned, and have not correctly calculated out the risk-benefit ratio of the operation they are about to perform. If I'm in a surgical situation where I'm getting nervous, it's a warning sign that I probably never should have been there in the first place.

The same is true of flying an airplane. If I'm an experienced pilot and I've flown five thousand times, and I'm getting ready to fly from Los Angeles to Beijing, even if there's turbulence, even if there's a storm, even if Beijing is fogged in, I'll know exactly what to do. I'm confident, not nervous.

If I see a nervous pilot climb into the cockpit, I'm looking for a way to get off the flight before we leave the ground. On the other hand, even though I don't want to fly with the nervous pilot, I don't want the cocky pilot at the controls either. And for neurosurgeons, that is the crux of the problem: The line between ego and confidence is too easily crossed.

Being a great technical neurosurgeon is never enough. In neurosurgery, good doctors require a combination of natural technical skills, intellect, training, experience, and the ability to remain humble in the face of the true awe and danger of working within the human brain. This is an essential concept every new neurosurgeon needs to learn, and one I do my best to convey to the young residents under my mentorship.

I recently went over our upcoming cases with two of our neurosurgery residents, and posed a question to them that was designed to teach this very lesson. We were in the radiology reading room, looking at the MRI scans of a twenty-three-year-old UCLA student under my care. She had been diagnosed with a benign tumor associated with a cyst growing inside her brain stem. The small, slow-growing tumor nodule was producing fluid, which resulted in the large cyst that was causing pressure in her brain stem and threatening her life.

"How would you treat this patient and manage her tumor?" I asked. "Confer between yourselves and then we'll talk about it."

The two young neurosurgeons huddled to ponder my question, then came back to me with their response. Roger, a brash young guy, was confident he could find safe passage along a lateral plane into the brain stem and thus extract the tumor. Andrew, the more cautious of the two, had been concerned that any effort to enter the brain stem would devastate if not kill the patient. After some deliberation between them, however, Roger won over his more conservative colleague. He convinced Andrew that the surgery would be possible using the approach he was proposing. They presented the plan to me.

I listened without comment. Then Andrew asked, "Well, what are *you* going to do?"

"I'm going to think about it," I replied, "and then I'm going to follow the best course of treatment for the patient."

That wasn't good enough for them, and they pressed me further. They insisted on knowing how I was going to get the tumor out.

"I'm not," I said flatly. "I'm not even going to try."

"I don't understand," Roger said.

"My point exactly. Any attempt to remove the tumor would carry too much risk for the patient. Removing it could leave her paralyzed, unable to speak, or in a coma. More importantly, the tumor is not the problem. It's very slow growing," I explained. "It's the cyst that is causing the problems for this patient. I'm going to put a needle in the cyst and drain it. That should relieve the immediate pressure, as well as her symptoms. We know that the tumor has been growing inside this young woman's brain stem for years," I explained. "It might take ten more years for it to grow big enough to cause symptoms. By that time, maybe we will have found something else for her in the way of treatment."

"But . . ." Roger began.

I interrupted him before he could continue. "The odds are that any surgical attempt to remove her tumor now will almost certainly leave her with new and potentially devastating deficits," I said. "Always remember to do what is best for the patient, and not a fancy surgery just to see if you can pull if off." Then I turned to Andrew. "Don't get buffaloed so easily," I said. "People who argue best aren't always right."

Most young neurosurgeons come out of their residency programs full of fighter-pilot bravado. They believe they can conquer the world, and every brain tumor as well. Being bold and swashbuckling and going for the heroic and difficult operation is not always the best thing for the patient, especially when the risks are high. The brain stem is an anatomical minefield for surgery; the risks of operating in this area are extremely high. It was where I dared not venture with Gerard Kelly, but Roger had so much confidence in his own ability that he thought he could pull it off.

Roger's audacity bordered on recklessness, and was of great concern to me, because it is my responsibility to make sure that these young brain surgeons don't learn the hard way that there are certain things they just can't do. It's my job to make sure that my residents become more than just technically proficient neurosurgeons. They need to become thoughtful warriors in the brain, doctors who are both knowledgeable enough and cautious enough to take only absolutely necessary risks for their patients.

The way to do that is to make sure they treat every patient as if that person were a loved one of their own—a child, a parent, a wife or husband. I told the parents of that twenty-three-year-old young woman with the cyst in her brain stem that I was treating their daughter exactly the way I would treat my own daughter, and I was absolutely sincere. Bonding with your patient on a personal level is the difference between being just a good technical neurosurgeon and being a truly great one. I believe that some neurosurgeons are born with more ability to empathize than others, and when I see that ability to deeply connect with the patient, I nurture it as much as possible. In those who lack that connection, I repeatedly emphasize strongly how necessary it is, which is why I was so stern with Roger.

In brain surgery, the slightest act of dehumanizing bravado can be devastating. When you are in the OR, if you do not possess compassion for your patients—if you don't have the ability to see them as members of your own family—then you are going to hurt them. I don't care how great a technical dissection you've done; there is a living, breathing human being attached to that tumor, and you are going to have to talk to the family of that person when you come out of surgery.

Becoming a great neurosurgeon cannot entirely be taught. I have seen doctors who are equally intelligent, with equally fine motor skills, same school, same residency . . . but one is an excellent surgeon, and one is not. There is a point at which a neurosurgeon must make the transition from technical-intellectual know-how to an intuitive understanding of what to do and when to stop.

Going back to fighter-pilot terms, how do I know to fly just at the edge of the envelope? How do I know where that edge lies? How can I determine whether making one extra cut will get the tumor out and cure the patient, or whether it will leave a person devastated? It is a subjective, seat-of-the-pants awareness that grows with repetition and time in the OR, but it is extremely hard to teach in the traditional sense. Trying to impart this knowledge academically is like teaching pilots to land an F-14 on the rolling deck of an aircraft carrier by handing them the flight manual.

I call this awareness "being focused"; athletes call it being "in the zone," but they are both manifestations of the same phenomenon. It comes from a part of your own brain that does not surface to full consciousness, but nevertheless informs your decision-making from the subconscious. When I am working in the brain, I need everyone participating in the surgery to be in the zone, with their full attention on the patient. This is why I don't play music in the operating room. I don't want my surgical team in Mozart's zone; I need them to be in mine. When we are all focused, coordination among team members just flows, often without anyone saying a word.

As surgeons, we may be in command in the OR, but not all decisions are made unilaterally. Deciding on what is best for the patient is a leading topic of conversation at our weekly Tumor Board meetings. The board is made up of me and the other doctors who are involved in the treatment of brain tumors, including the neuroradiologist, the radiation oncologist, the neuro-oncologist, and the neuropathologist. Although the constitution changes from one week to another, usually there are about ten physicians around the table. Members of the nursing staff, residents, and others involved in patient care may also be present.

We convene to discuss various treatment options for each patient, and I encourage those who have firm opinions to speak up in our meetings, even if they dissent from the prevailing point of view. Everyone has a chance to make his or her case and convince the rest of the group. Usually, we come to consensus. If not, we take our split decision to the patient.

The patient always has the final say. I emphasize this point many times over: We work for the patient; patients don't work for us. People with brain tumors come to us because we are a team of experts. If all our experts are in agreement on a course of treatment, there will be a unanimous decision from the Tumor Board, but even then the patient still may say no.

I include our residents in the Tumor Board meetings because I want them to see that there are many possible ways to fight brain tumors, and that highly qualified people can disagree in a forum that is focused solely on the best possible outcome for the patient. Phil Moore, a second-year resident at Cedars-Sinai, feels that the Tumor Board meetings are truly "translational," or multidisciplinary, and that younger neurosurgeons such as himself, who may have been trained to see surgery as the best possible option for a patient, are forced to recognize multiple other possibilities. "When you listen to several men you respect—an oncologist, a radiologist, a research scientist—and hear them making different cases for different options in a particular case, it can make you feel pretty humble," he admits. "I've learned that surgery is not always the best option."

For our residents, finding that intuitive focus and becoming the accomplished thief in the night can lead to marvelous surgical results, but that too can lead to problems of another sort. I have a responsibility to see that my young neurosurgeons do not get too full of themselves and fall victim to the God complex. In this effort I try to lead by example. I very rarely read magazine articles that are written about me. When I complete a complex operation, I never pat myself on the back for very long. I give myself four or five seconds to be happy about it, then I very deliberately turn the page and move on.

After a successful surgery, appreciative patients and their families sometimes say, "You're God," or "You're an angel." I know they intend it as high praise, and I know that it springs from joyful gratitude. Nevertheless, it makes me extremely uncomfortable to hear it, so much so that I almost literally shut my ears. I don't want to listen because I know the danger that comes from believing it.

If you start buying into the hype and the flattery and the fluff, it's a slippery slope that can easily carry you over the border from confidence into arrogance. Hubris is not only toxic, it can be deadly. If I ever let down my guard and allow myself to get overconfident or cocky, I'm going to miss a step, lose my focus, and then I'm going to hurt somebody.

We need to recognize our limitations and stay humble. Surgeons love to operate. That's what we're trained for. But as was demonstrated by the case of the brain-stem tumor that I discussed with Roger and Andrew, surgery is not always the way to go. Sometimes, doing what's best for the patient means knowing when *not* to operate, or when to back off during an operation.

Milagros Reid is one such patient. Her case demonstrates how restraint can be the difference between success and failure—or life and death.

"Look at me!" exclaimed Milagros Reid with a twinkle when I met her for the first time. "Here I am—at the celebrity hospital!" She was wearing a broad smile, faded black jeans, and an aloha shirt.

A vibrant, vigorous woman of sixty-six, her first symptom a year earlier had been a momentary dizzy spell that caught her by surprise while she was backpacking her way through New Zealand. The oldest of twelve children born on the family farm at the base of the volcanic Mount Pinatubo in the Philippines, Ms. Reid had always been an adventurer. She and her husband, a naval officer, had lived all over the world, and she was not afraid to go out on her own in search of experiences that might seem intimidating even to a younger person. She had mistakenly attributed that first dizzy spell to the bottled water she had bought in a market near the hostel where she was staying in New Zealand.

When she returned to southern California to her home in nearby Pasadena, she experienced her first actual seizure, which was initially misdiagnosed as a stroke. The next seizure took away her speech before rendering her unconscious. She emerged from the episode with her speech intact, but this time a CT scan revealed a tumor in the left frontal lobe of her brain, adjacent to the critical language area, requiring an awake craniotomy.

It was this finding that had prompted her daughter to search the Internet for a tumor center, which led her to us at Cedars. An alert, intelligent woman with a charming sense of humor, Ms. Reid appeared to be an excellent candidate for an awake craniotomy.

For a patient this surely sounds like a daunting prospect, but I needed Milagros to be awake and responsive on the operating table for a portion of her surgery—with her brain exposed. I had to pinpoint the precise location of her tumor in relation to her language area so that I would not damage it in the course of her operation. To do that, Milagros would be roused from her general anesthetic so she could answer questions from our neurologist, Dr. Dawn Eliashiv. At the same time, I would place and stimulate electrodes directly on her brain to map out her language area.

The language area is a crucial part of the brain, and it does far more than furnish us with the power of speech. It also gives us the ability to understand language, both written and spoken, and to make sense of the world around us. If you lose that ability, it is devastating. You become not just someone who is unable to speak, but someone who is unable to identify common objects. Damage to the language area is perhaps the most devastating neurological injury that a person can have.

The awake craniotomy originated half a century ago with pioneering neurosurgeon Wilder Penfield. He was a protégé of Harvey Cushing, the man considered to be the father of neuroscience. Penfield developed the technique to help patients with severe epilepsy. Why did the patient have to be awake? Because every brain is unique.

The human brain is like a face. Faces have general features in common—eyes, nose, lips—but every face has its own distinct characteristics. Our brains are organized topographically, with motor areas, sensory areas, visual areas, and language areas. All brains are arranged in the same general way, but like faces, they are not identical. Each person's "brainscape" is different, and because there is so much variability from one person to another, we cannot assume that a patient's language is in a particular spot based only on a generalized road map, or even on that individual's pre-surgical MRI scan. Moreover, with bilingual and multilingual patients, it is not unusual for one language to be stored in one area of the brain, and the second language to reside in an adjacent area.

Milagros Reid would not experience any pain during her surgery. The brain itself has no sensation—it can't feel a thing. We would anesthetize her scalp for the duration of the operation; she would only be awake for about an hour at the most. Dr. Ray Chu and I were to be her co-surgeons. From her pre-op functional MRI scan, I was concerned about the unfavorable location of the tumor, which appeared to be located dangerously close to her language area. Although I believed that Milagros Reid would do well answering questions on the operating table, I was acutely aware that if the tumor did not lie outside her language area, we would not be able to take it out.

Because of the suspicious location of her tumor, her question-and-answer session with Dr. Eliashiv was especially important. Dr. Eliashiv would be looking for what is called language arrest. As I stimulated areas of her brain with the electrodes, if Milagros faltered, failed to respond to questions from Dr. Eliashiv, or could not identify common objects correctly, we would then know that the area of the brain being stimulated was important to language function. One common type of language arrest is called perseveration, in which the patient repeats the answer to the last question rather than giving the correct answer to the current question.

Ms. Reid's wake-up call in surgery went exactly according to plan. Twenty minutes after the anesthesia was halted, she was awake and responsive, answering Dr. Eliashiv's questions, while I began the task of mapping out her language.

We suspected that Ms. Reid's tumor was an astrocytoma, but we would not know for sure until we got the pathology results. Astrocytoma tumor cells are star-shaped, and these tumors can range from slow-growing Grade 1 or 2 tumors, which are considered pre-cancerous, to fast-growing Grade 4 tumors, which are considered highly malignant. A Grade 4 astrocytoma is the same tumor as a glioblastoma multiforme, which is most often fatal.

We believed that Milagros's tumor was a low-grade, slow-growing astrocytoma because we had seen no enhancement—no pickup of dye—on the pre-operative MRI. If there had been, it would have been indicative of potential malignancy. This figured prominently in our risk-benefit calculation. Because of where the tumor was located, we already knew that the odds of achieving an image-complete resection were against us. If this was indeed a slow-growing tumor, causing a vital person like Milagros Reid any language deficit while removing it would have been unacceptable.

It was imperative to map out Milagros's entire language area before making any attempt to go after the tumor. The prevailing surgical standard in such cases calls for maintaining a one-centimeter margin between the tumor and the language area, as evidenced by our mapping, but I was willing to settle for less of a margin as long as we had a clean separation—a good surgical plane to follow between the two.

Unfortunately, once we began I could see no clear opening to Ms. Reid's tumor. There was no easy, distinct plane for the thief in the night to proceed along. Moreover, my first attempts to stimulate the area sent her stumbling into perseveration. It became obvious that the tumor had invaded her language area.

We had what was clearly a no-go situation. The decision to proceed or stand down had become a numbers game, and the chips were stacked against us. The risk of leaving Ms. Reid with significant language deficit was getting into the 15 to 20 percent range, which is unacceptable for the removal of what we suspected was a low-grade astrocytoma. At that point Ray and I decided that it was in the patient's best interest for us not to attempt to remove the tumor. Her seizures could be controlled by medication, and we would deal with the tumor itself by nonsurgical means.

I had just finished mapping out language and was ready to turn the closure over to Dr. Chu when pathologist Serguei Bannykh entered the operating room with the preliminary results from the first biopsy specimens. His findings matched our initial analysis. Milagros Reid had a low-grade oligoastrocytoma. The final lab report a week later confirmed it.

We have found that this low-grade oligo-type tumor responds very well to the chemotherapy agent Temodar (temozolomide). Milagros would probably have another five to seven years of quality life, and the possibility of many more good years beyond that, depending on a more detailed genetic analysis of the tumor.

You never really know what you're dealing with until the science reveals it to you. Whether we choose to do surgery or arrive at some other treatment plan, it often comes down to a strategic calculation based on the individual's particular situation. If analysis had revealed that Milagros Reid's tumor was a malignant glioblastoma and she had two months to live without an image-complete resection, it might have tipped the scales more in favor of proceeding with surgery. What always controls the risk-benefit analysis is quite simply and quite finally to do what is best for the patient.

Beyond knowing textbook neuroanatomy, neurophysiology, and techniques of neurosurgery, there is an energy, a spiritual flow between doctor and patient that is essential in an outstanding neurosurgeon. Patients may not always be able to articulate it, but they generally can feel this spiritual connection when it exists. This ability to merge your skill and expertise with your empathy and compassion is the key to becoming a thoughtful warrior in the brain. And, I would submit, without the mind-set of the thoughtful warrior, it is very difficult to become an expert thief in the night.

Sadly, becoming the expert thief in the night in the operating room is seldom enough. In treating brain cancer, tumor surgery is usually the beginning, not the end, because many tumors regrow. As a result, neurosurgeons coordinate with a wide range of other medical specialists. At Cedars we have expanded this coordination to include not just physicians involved with patient care, but researchers working in the lab as well. By opening the feedback loop between the lab and the hospital, breakthroughs in one area inform research and treatment in the other. This is vital to our work, and is at the heart of what we call our translational, or "bench-to-bedside," approach. One innovation resulting from this partnership between research and patient care is a promising vaccine against brain cancer, and my patient Glenn Rhoades was among the first to receive it.

CHAPTER 5

Outsmarting the Tumor

We had a saying back in the 1980s, when I was a resident at the University of Michigan. After removing a malignant brain tumor, someone in the OR would announce, "Okay, we're ready for the ATJ." ATJ stood for "Anti-Tumor Juice," and it was entirely wishful thinking on our part. We were hoping that one day a substance would come along to kill off the residual cancer cells that we knew we had left behind in the patient's brain—even in the most successful of surgeries. Dr. Glenn Kindt, one of my professors, was the originator of the saying, but for all of us—and for our patients—that day couldn't come soon enough. As it turns out, for my patient Glenn Rhoades, and for others as well, "soon enough" may be here.

"Was I funny again this time?" Glenn Rhoades asked, grinning as I lifted his bandage and examined the sutures from his surgery. It had been only a day since his operation, but he was already healing well and seemed in excellent spirits.

"No," I answered, smiling back at him. "You slept through this one, just the way you were supposed to."

Glenn Rhoades was recovering from his second brain operation in three years. His first tumor had been situated in his left frontal lobe, near Broca's area. Named for nineteenth-century French physician Paul Broca, the area controls language processing, speech production, and comprehension. Given the tumor's location, Glenn's initial surgery was an awake craniotomy. I needed him to respond to questions in the OR, much like Milagros Reid had done during her operation. Apparently, however, the seat of Glenn's lively sense of humor is nowhere near Broca's area, because even though sedated he was cracking jokes throughout the awake portion of the procedure.

Because the language fibers in Broca's area run deep and connect to other language areas in the temporal lobe, Glenn had a lot of talking to do during his operation. It was not something we asked him to do, but as the electrodes stimulated him, he apparently pulled a page out of his old high school biology textbook and began reciting all the scientific classifications of the animal world: domain, kingdom, phylum, class, order, family, genus, and species—in order.

This was pretty much unique in my surgical experience, and I asked him whether he knew why he'd done it. "I don't have a clue," he replied with a shrug. "They just started coming to me, and I began ticking them off out loud. I also recall someone in the operating room saying, 'I didn't know that.' I actually remember the discussion."

Later on, I told him he was funny, and at one of his follow-up visits to the clinic he described what the experience of the awake craniotomy had been like for him. Glenn had an uncommonly clear recollection of his surgery. "The whole process was just bizarre," he told me. "My face seemed to be peeled forward, and your neurologist was trying to show me these pictures. I didn't have any physical sensation of pain, but I knew I was in some weird situation, because my skull was all pinned down with rods everywhere."

That initial surgery had gone quite well. We achieved an image-complete resection, and the pathology report revealed that the tumor we removed was a low-grade oligodendroglioma. Oligodendrogliomas are slow-growing tumors of the supportive or glial tissue of the brain. They are most commonly found in middle-aged men and women, but because they grow so slowly, it is often the case that they have been present in the brain for many years before being discovered.

Glenn Rhoades's first tumor was found quite by accident. An observant colleague sitting opposite him in his office one day happened to notice that the pupil of one eye seemed larger than the other. "He was looking across at me and he said, 'Your pupils don't look the same,'" Glenn recalled. "I popped up and went to the bathroom and sure enough, my right pupil was dilated."

A visit to the ophthalmologist led to a chain of referrals, an MRI scan, and the diagnosis that a virus had attacked the papillary response nerve in his right eye. The uneven pupils had absolutely nothing to do with his tumor, but they were the reason for his original MRI. Finding the tumor was a fluke. "I was on the way back to the neurologist," he told me during our first meeting. "I pulled out the MRIs in the parking lot, and you didn't need any special training to see this huge tumor in my left frontal lobe."

Like many of my patients, Glenn Rhoades had found me on the Internet. A local physician in the San Diego area had recommended that he undergo a surgical biopsy first to learn what kind of tumor he had, but my advice to him at our first meeting was to skip the biopsy. "We don't know what this is," I said to him, "but it's got to come out." He agreed.

In my experience, taking the "conservative" approach and doing a surgical biopsy is not necessarily the best choice. If I know the tumor is growing, and if I know it has to be removed, a biopsy only puts the patient through an additional surgical procedure, with all of its attendant risks. Moreover, performing a biopsy and extracting limited tissue samples may not tell the whole story. Tumors are not necessarily uniform throughout; beyond the small section removed for biopsy, other parts of the tumor may already be cancerous. If you do a limited biopsy and tell the patient that everything is fine, a few months later he or she may come back with a tumor that is far more advanced.

And far more dangerous. Unfortunately, the majority of benign tumors don't stay that way. Over time, approximately 70 percent of low-grade, noncancerous tumors will eventually morph into higher-grade, more aggressive tumors. This malignant transformation is perhaps the most compelling reason of all to skip the biopsy and simply remove the tumor.

Starting with our initial meeting, Glenn had more than a passing interest in the possible environmental causes of his tumor. As we talked, it seemed to me that his entire childhood and young adult life in southern California yielded up a multitude of potential contributing factors. Glenn grew up in the 1960s in the community of Riverside, fifty miles inland from Los Angeles. Before there was mandatory air pollution control, prevailing westerly winds blew southern California's rapidly increasing quantity of automotive exhaust fumes and airborne industrial waste toward Riverside. The town is nestled at the base of the San Gabriel mountains and the pollutants collected there, trapped near ground level by the inversion layer and by local geography. They were then "cooked" by sunlight into an even more noxious red-brown brew. Riverside at the time had some of the worst air quality in the region, particularly in the warm summer months.

This is, of course, when kids spend more time out of doors. After school was out for the summer, Glenn and his pals earned spending money by mowing lawns around town—when the air was at its most toxic levels. "My friends and I used to call it 'getting smogged,'" he recalled. "That was when you had exerted yourself so much on a polluted day that you could no longer inhale comfortably. Your lungs just ached. In those days, moms didn't drive kids from place to place. We all got around on our bikes. And we just kept going until we got smogged. Once I had to stop halfway through mowing a lawn. I was no longer able to continue. The guy whose house it was had to drive me home. It just hurt too much to breathe."

His description made me cringe, but it was only one of many potential contributing factors in his history. Back then, people were only beginning to be concerned about environmental hazards to the human body. During the summers, Glenn took advanced placement science classes in the summer program at his high school. Students were permitted to handle a wide array of extremely hazardous chemicals—everything from raw mercury to highly corrosive ammonium hydroxide—without appropriate safety attire. Such unprotected proximity to poisonous chemicals would never be allowed today.

"I was exposed to all kinds of stuff," Glenn admitted. "After my parents painted the house with leaded oil-based paint, I woke up with a sore throat every day for weeks. And my friends and I never gave a second thought to cleaning the parts from our motorcycles in a big bowl of gasoline with our bare hands," he added. "Then we would take our boats and go scuba diving on the rock-covered outfall pipeline from the San Diego sewer system—because that's where the abalone were."

As he got older, he became much more careful about his health. "I stopped smoking and drinking in 1984, and I started exercising and eating right. And today I can't buy swordfish at Costco without seeing a warning label telling me to limit my consumption." Glenn now lives with his longtime domestic partner, Carol, in the seaside town of Carlsbad in north San Diego County, where the air quality is uniformly excellent. Now in his midfifties, he recently retired from his highly successful position as an information technology executive, but he still rides a motorcycle. He and Carol take frequent recreational trips on the bike up and down the coast—that is, when he isn't racing his sports car.

Glenn Rhoades is an avid amateur sports car racing enthusiast, and travels around the west from one contest to another. Within three weeks after his initial surgery, he was back on his bike and behind the wheel of his racecar. He always came in for regular checkups, and for two and a half years his MRIs were negative—there was no evidence of tumor regrowth.

Last year he stopped in with Carol for his scheduled MRI on the way to the big automobile show in Las Vegas. This time I had to tell him that the news was not altogether positive. "The film is showing some regrowth of the tumor," I said.

Good or bad, I always state the news as calmly and straightforwardly as possible. A high percentage of these tumors regrow, even after an image-complete resection. Glenn took it philosophically, as if he had known all along that this day would come, and he had already resigned himself to it. “Okay,” he said without hesitation, his boyish smile setting the room at ease, “when do you want to do the surgery?”

This was Glenn Rhoades, the delegator. “My pattern for success my whole life has been that if I don’t feel I’m the expert at something, I find the guy who is,” he said simply. “And then I do what they say, and I don’t spend a lot of time second-guessing them.”

After the tumor was discovered, he had done his research and found his team, and we were it. Exactly as he had countless times in the business world, from the beginning he had handed over all decisions about his care to my staff and me. He just signed the consent forms and got ready to let us do our best to remove the second tumor a few weeks later.

This time there was no need to awaken Glenn during the operation. The regrowth was not in the language area, so we would be deprived of his sense of humor in the OR. For the second time, however, I was able to achieve an image-complete resection, which was good news indeed. Now, here he was, one day out of his second surgery.

“So . . . it’s another low-grade tumor?” he asked hopefully.

Every new tumor patient is thrust into a flurry of unfamiliar medical terms and phrases. Many tumor names are polysyllabic tongue-twisters, and the way they are classified is perhaps confusing, at least at first. Tumors are graded on the basis of their malignancy. Grade 1 is considered the least malignant, and Grade 4 is the most malignant. Grade 1 tumors have distinct borders, and are sometimes called benign. They may not grow at all, or grow only very slowly. More rapidly growing tumors are sometimes called infiltrating tumors, and are classified as either low-grade, intermediate-grade, or high-grade (Grades 3 through 4). What determines the grade is how fast the tumor is growing, whether new blood vessels are forming to feed it, and whether areas of the tumor are growing faster than its ability to grow new blood vessels, causing areas of the tumor to die from a lack of blood supply, which is called necrosis. What this does not take into account, however, is the tumor's location. A Grade 1 "benign" tumor in the wrong location, such as pressing on the brain stem, can be every bit as deadly as a Grade 4 malignancy.

"The initial biopsy reports look good," I replied. "We didn't see anything higher than a Grade 2, but we'll have to wait for the final pathology before we know for certain what we're dealing with."

I already had my suspicions, however, that we weren't dealing with another low-grade growth. Glenn's pre-surgery MRIs were showing some enhancement, meaning the tumor was taking up dye. This suggested it may have progressed to a higher grade—a malignancy.

"Are you feeling a little more yourself today?" I asked as I moved his skull bandage back and looked at his sutures.

"Yes," he said. "I guess if I'm going to get a brain tumor, this is the one to get. Even if it does come back."

"Your family came by?" I asked, already knowing the answer.

"Absolutely," Glenn replied. "My son is the real checkpoint about how I'm doing. We have a deal—after surgery he needs me to recite something arcane, something that proves to him that I can still think. This time, as soon as he and Carol walked in to say hello, I said, '0325235*.' "

"What is that?" I asked.

"It's the code to our storage unit, where we keep the racing parts."

Outside his room, Suzane Brian reviewed Glenn's labs with me. His electrolytes were in balance. His white blood count was a little elevated, due to the steroids we were giving him to decrease his brain swelling. He was also on an anti-seizure medication, as well as Zantac—whenever you administer steroids after surgery, you have to give the patient something to protect the stomach. His post-surgical MRI looked perfect—no sign of residual tumor. I was still concerned about the final pathology report, but there was no sense causing unnecessary alarm. Mr. Rhoades, a veteran of two brain tumor surgeries, had been through enough already. I was hoping he would have a steady ride from here on. I would know more in several days, when I read the final biopsy reports.

Unfortunately, the news at the end of the week was not good. His final pathology reports came back indicating that the recurrence of his low-grade tumor from three years ago had in fact become malignant—a Grade 3 anaplastic astrocytoma. Grade 3 astrocytomas have a tendency to recur quickly and are considered cancerous. Glenn Rhoades would be getting additional treatment, including chemotherapy, radiation, and possibly our tumor vaccine program.

By the time I was a resident, we'd already come a long way since the early days of brain surgery pioneers Harvey Cushing and Wilder Penfield, but it was clear even then that if we were to have any real impact on long-term survival, we were going to have to go beyond the surgical debulking process. We knew we would have to go after these tumors with much more targeted weaponry, on a cellular, molecular, and genetic level.

I already knew this when I arrived at UCLA in 1987 as an assistant professor in the division of neurosurgery. I was thirty, fresh from my neurosurgical residency at the University of Michigan. It was an exciting time for me. I came in as head of the brain tumor program, and I was busy in the lab. I already had my first National Institutes of Health research grant to study brain edema, or swelling in the brain.

The roots of this research went back to my earliest days at Michigan. I was eighteen when I began working in the lab of Dr. Donald Weidler at the Upjohn Research

Center; we were trying to figure out a way to protect the brain from stroke damage. We found that in animals we could reduce the amount of brain damage from a stroke by 60 to 70 percent if we put them into a barbiturate-induced coma. This was done by administering phenobarbital within three hours of the onset of the stroke, and it prevented much of the brain cell death resulting from stroke.

It was groundbreaking work, but the method—inducing a barbiturate coma—was extreme. The doses of barbiturates required for the coma were very high, and there was considerable risk of life-threatening side effects. In humans, phenobarbital in sufficient quantity to render a patient comatose could also be enough to stop the heart or result in a dangerous drop in blood pressure. Most physicians were understandably reluctant to put patients in a barbiturate coma, except as a treatment of last resort to halt life-threatening brain swelling.

I was still at Michigan when I began looking for a safer way of protecting the brain after a stroke, and I came up with the idea of using fish oil. Today fish oil and omega-3 pills are common nutritional supplements, and people are routinely encouraged to add deep-water fish to their diets, but back then their popularity was still fifteen years off. I suspected that fish oil would work because I had read that native Inuit people of Greenland, whose diet consisted largely of whale blubber, seldom suffered heart attacks or strokes. Knowing that whale blubber is high in omega-3 fatty acids—the beneficial component in fish or fish oil—I began feeding rats omega-3 fish oil. When I induced strokes in these rats, the result was a dramatic 50 to 70 percent reduction in post-stroke brain cell death.

At about the same time, the Swedish researcher Bengt Samuelsson won a Nobel Prize for his landmark finding that leukotrienes, which are molecules found in white blood cells, could cause inflammation in the lungs. It struck me that leukotrienes might also be a cause of brain swelling, which is all too common in the aftermath of brain tumors, strokes, and head trauma. Eventually I was able to show a direct correlation between the amount of swelling around the tumors and the amount of leukotrienes present in the tumors. Finally, I demonstrated that if I administered a drug that blocked leukotriene formation, I could prevent brain swelling.

At Michigan I published a number of journal articles on the subject. The discovery garnered considerable attention within the scientific community, and I was invited as a special guest at national and international scientific meetings to present my findings. My research career was off to a spectacular start.

Or so it seemed. When I arrived at UCLA with a huge NIH grant to take my findings to the next level, I ran into a nasty little problem: I couldn't duplicate my own research.

When I tried to reproduce my Michigan experiments by injecting leukotrienes into the brains of rats, there was no edema. Maybe the leukotrienes had gone bad, I thought, so I repeated the experiments with freshly made doses of leukotrienes. That was not the problem. Nothing seemed to be the problem—I could not figure out what the glitch was. There I was, with all these published papers "proving" that leukotrienes caused brain swelling, having made special presentations at international meetings on brain edema and strokes, with a multimillion-dollar NIH grant, my own independent laboratory at UCLA—and I couldn't reproduce my own experiment.

It was beyond embarrassing. I envisioned the disgrace and the loss of reputation that would result from the next round of scientific papers I would have to write, retracting my already published findings. Careers had been ruined on far less. What I did not realize at the time was that a door to a much more important discovery was about to open, and that I would soon be holding the key to unlocking the previously impermeable blood-brain barrier.

The blood-brain barrier is both a physical and a biochemical barrier inside the walls of the capillaries in the brain. It is unique to the capillaries in the brain, and it is one of the brain's most important protectors. The capillaries of the brain are very different from capillaries anywhere else in the body. Capillaries in other parts of the body are porous, with little gaps between cells. Like garden soaker hoses, they allow water, glucose, proteins, nutrients, and medications to freely trickle out of the bloodstream and into the adjacent tissue. In science we actually describe them as "leaky capillaries." Capillaries in the brain are not constructed that way. They are impermeable, and prevent anything that is water soluble from percolating out into the brain.

This is the blood-brain barrier, and it is absolutely critical to life. The reason why it is important is that the brain is in some respects nothing more than a very highly regulated electrical box, with electrical activity being controlled by the chemicals that are in the brain. Without the blood-brain barrier, every time we ate a meal, chemicals from the food we ingested would seep out into the tissues of the brain. The fluctuations would cause havoc, short-circuiting our delicate electrical and biochemical machinery.

Even water cannot get across the blood-brain barrier. Only drugs that can be dissolved in oil, or lipids, can cross it. This includes morphine and various antidepressants and antipsychotic medications, which are very lipid soluble, but most chemotherapeutic drugs are not. This is not a problem provided you are in good health, but it's really bad if you have a brain tumor and we are trying to get drugs into the brain to treat it. About 98 percent of the drugs that could be therapeutically useful in the brain are water soluble, and thus cannot get across this blood-brain barrier. Historically this has presented a huge problem: When we administered chemotherapy, we have not been able to get the drugs into the brain tumor in high enough concentrations to make an impact.

What does this have to do with my leukotriene research? And why wasn't I able to reproduce the breakdown of the blood-brain barrier and get the resulting swelling? The problem, I finally realized, was my increased proficiency. By the time I arrived at UCLA, I had gotten much better at injecting the leukotrienes into the rat brains—I was not causing any injury to the surface of the brain the way I had in the Michigan experiments.

When I re-created the experiments exactly as I had done them at Michigan, allowing the high-speed dental drill I was using to open the skull to get hot and cause a heat injury to the rat brain, the injection of leukotrienes caused the capillaries to become leaky. This produced the edema, or swelling of the brain, I'd been looking for, but only in the area of the heat-injured brain. Without that brain injury, there was no breakdown in the blood-brain barrier—the capillaries in the rest of the brain did not become leaky. This was a huge clue: Normal brain could resist the effects of leukotrienes, but damaged brain could not, resulting in a breakdown of the blood-brain barrier.

I then injected leukotrienes into the brains of rats with brain tumors. Only the capillaries in the brain tumors became leaky, while the capillaries in the normal brain surrounding the tumor were absolutely unaffected by the leukotrienes. I concluded that leukotrienes could cause brain swelling or leaky capillaries only in areas where the brain was already damaged or diseased, but not in normal, healthy brain. This was a major breakthrough—I had for the first time selectively opened the blood-brain barrier in brain tumors.

I had stumbled on a way to circumvent one of the most difficult obstacles to treating disease in the brain. By making brain capillaries in the area of brain tumors leaky, it would allow a whole range of beneficial water soluble drugs to reach tumors or diseased tissue. At the same time, capillaries in the normal brain would remain intact. This would prevent drugs from getting into the normal brain tissue, where they could cause side effects or damage.

As had been the case when I was in high school many years prior, when I had noticed porcupine-shaped echinocyte blood cells in patients who had been on the heart-lung bypass machine, the pursuit of the "odd observation" had paid off in a major way. In that case, the need to incubate red blood cells overnight at body temperature accidentally revealed a crucial deformity the next morning. In this instance, I had started out attempting to study brain swelling, and inadvertently discovered the key to selectively opening the blood-brain barrier in brain tumors. Such unexpected breakthroughs are among the greatest joys in the life of a scientist. Good scientists must be able to focus on the observations that challenge the very basis of their hypotheses, and sometimes we make the biggest discoveries by accident.

I continued at UCLA, dividing my time between the OR and the research lab. By 1997, I had been there for a decade. I had a busy neurosurgical practice, a prestigious endowed chair, and my own research laboratory with federal grants from the National Institutes of Health for my lab research. I was even doing early work on a brain cancer vaccine. I had spent my entire career in the ivory towers, and everything was going according to schedule. Within academia there was a well-trodden path you expected to follow. You go to a great medical school, get into an outstanding neurosurgery training program, become chief resident, then get a university appointment and move up the tenure-track ladder—assistant professor, associate professor, full professor—until finally becoming chairman of the department.

At the age of thirty-nine, I was one rung from the top. I'd become one of the youngest full professors ever in the department of surgery at UCLA; the next step up would be to become head of the department. It was unclear, however, whether that would happen at UCLA. I was now at a point in my career where I'd caught the attention of several other neurosurgery centers. I was being recruited to move elsewhere, and was on the short list of candidates to become chairman of neurosurgery at Harvard's Massachusetts General Hospital, at Stanford University, and at the University of California at San Francisco.

I was right on track in one sense, but something was still missing. Becoming chairman of neurosurgery did not mean as much to me as finding a cure for brain tumors. I wanted to find a way to create a spectacular state-of-the-art center for bench-to-bedside translational research. What is translational research? We already knew that surgery was not going to be the answer, that we would need weapons to outsmart the tumor that had been developed in the lab. My idea was to bring what we were learning in the lab—the bench—to the treatment arena—the bedside. Conversely, we would be able to take what we were learning at the bedside and bring it back into the lab to readjust and improve the treatment. This continuous feedback loop from bench to bedside and back to bench would greatly accelerate the learning process, giving patients their best chance for long-term survival, and, I hoped, an eventual cure.

It sounds logical enough, but putting it into practice was another matter entirely. One problem in traditional academic medical research has always been the fundamental disconnect between the research scientists working in the labs and the physicians working with the patients. Bench and bedside exist in two parallel universes, or silos, if you will. In fact, they speak different languages. Their goals are entirely different, and in general there is very little communication between them.

The classically trained basic researcher is focused on finding a particular molecule or process, and then studying every aspect of that molecule or process, because that's the way the traditional funding mechanisms work. That molecule may hold the key to curing cancer, but researchers are not necessarily focused on trying to cure cancer;

they are focused on simply trying to understand how their molecule works.

They are often unlikely to make the transition from lab discovery to clinical application on any number of grounds. First, researchers don't generally have the expertise to understand the clinical issues involved in the treatment of cancer. Second, historically there has been no payoff for them to do so. Quite the opposite is the case: Going in that direction could cost them their funding if it doesn't work. Researchers are not going to risk getting funding cut off if they are doing very well getting their grants and learning how this molecule bends, turns, and binds to other molecules. That's the way 99 percent of academic researchers operate. That's the way that 99 percent of science operates.

Meanwhile, on the clinical side, physicians treating cancer patients have little or no understanding of the basic research going on in the laboratories, or that a molecule under investigation has the potential to become the next big advance against cancer. Clinicians are in the trenches, treating patients, waiting for the pharmaceutical companies to get FDA approval for new drugs they can add to their arsenal. They are not interested in trying to bring in a new molecule to treat cancer. They don't have the time or the expertise to do that.

I knew that between these two silos, there was a huge untapped opportunity to accelerate the science and bring it to bear in the war on brain cancer. I also knew this would be the best chance I had of gaining the upper hand against malignant brain tumors. I called it my Manhattan Project, after the intensive multidisciplinary effort by physicists, chemists, and other scientists to quickly develop the atomic bomb during World War II.

Early in 1997 I returned to my office one afternoon to learn from my assistant that Jerry Levey, the provost and dean of the Medical School, had called and wanted to set up a meeting. I wasn't surprised. It was no longer a secret that other medical schools had been recruiting me—when they get down to their final list of candidates, they start making calls and asking about you, and word gets out. Jerry was a physician who had chosen to leave the practice of medicine for a career as an administrator. I liked him and we got along well; he had always been very supportive of me. I had received accelerated promotions, and he saw that I got the lab research space I needed. As I made my way across the campus to his office, I had a good idea what he wanted to talk to me about that afternoon, and I was right.

"Keith," he began as we took our seats at the conference table in his large, wood-paneled office, "we've received inquiries, and I know you're being recruited by other institutions. What would it take to keep you here?"

He had opened the door. Now it was up to me. I asked him to give me a few days to think about it. He agreed.

I knew exactly what I wanted to have if I was to stay at UCLA. I wanted money to set up my Manhattan Project.

The potential was clearly there. Over the past ten years, Don Becker, chief of the division of neurosurgery, and I had taken the UCLA neurosurgery program from fifty to five hundred brain surgeries annually. The brain tumor center of excellence I would propose to Jerry Levey would attract far more patients, which could ultimately fund the building of the research team.

I knew I could make it pencil out, but I had to be able to prove it. I took $10,000 of my own money and retained the services of the former chief financial officer of UCLA, who was now with a private medical consulting firm. Together we drew up a detailed business plan for the Manhattan Project. We showed how we could create a comprehensive brain tumor center with state-of-the-art translational research and state-of-the-art clinical trials, with the focus on finding a cure for malignant brain tumors. The plan called for the hiring of one basic researcher, three research nurses to run the clinical trials and to interface with the FDA and the Institutional Review Board at UCLA, and a couple of data managers to follow up on all the data. An additional $2 million in projected hospital profits would offset the initial cost of the program as we attracted more brain tumor surgical patients to UCLA. What I needed was $750,000 in seed money to launch the program. I put together what I thought was a very compelling proposal, which I then sent over to Jerry Levey for his review.

A few days later, he called me to his office for another meeting. This time he brought in the hospital's chief executive officer as well. "Keith," Dr. Levey said, "we think you're great. If you come back with a plan for about $75,000 a year, we can make this work."

I was astonished. I'd been expecting him to come back with maybe $500,000. At $500,000, we could talk. There was nothing I could do with $75,000. Dejected, I went back to my office.

I was thirty-nine, and I figured that I had another ten or fifteen years to try to make a big impact in the war on brain cancer. Whenever I asked myself what I wanted to do, the answer always came back clear and immediate: I wanted to find cures. I didn't just want to continue moving up the academic ranks, doing traditional lab research, and performing surgery. We removed the tumors, but they just kept growing back.

I knew that the only way to accelerate the search for a cure was to take full advantage of the explosion of information coming in from the molecular/genetic revolution over the past decade, and to build a bridge connecting the silos of the researchers and the clinicians. I didn't want to wait another twenty years for this stuff to make its way into the treatment arena; I wanted to put it to use to save the lives of my patients as soon as possible.

As I reviewed my options at other institutions, I suddenly understood that it didn't matter. Wherever I went in academic medicine, it was going to be the same story. While neurosurgery is a profit center at most institutions, these profits seldom come back to the department for research. Instead, they are used to make up for red ink from other less profitable departments. Many nonsurgical medical center departments operate in the red, which means that profits from departments that do surgery and other procedures are used to underwrite departments that do not, like pediatrics and psychiatry. Of course, those departments have to survive; I was just asking for a portion of the revenue we would be generating so that we could make an impact on what I believe is the most significant organ in the body—the human brain.

But this wasn't going to happen—not at UCLA or anywhere else in academic medicine. I looked carefully at the chairmanships I was up for. When you get on the short list, you get to see the financials, and I could see that there was no research money to be had at any of them. There was no money at UCSF, no money at Stanford, no money at Harvard.

That meeting with Jerry Levey was an epiphany for me. I realized that I had gone as far as I could in a traditional academic environment. I was going to have to find another way to implement my Manhattan Project. If I was to have any impact on this disease, I needed a unique situation, a place with the financial resources and the infrastructure that could accommodate my translational bench-to-bedside approach. I picked up the phone and called Tom Priselac, the chief executive officer of Cedars-Sinai Medical Center.

In 1997, Cedars was already a very large private, nonprofit hospital. It had abundant clinical expertise, with two thousand physicians on staff. It had lots of space: An entire floor—eight operating rooms—could potentially be devoted to neurosurgery. It had a big research building and great lab facilities, and much of it was underused at the time. It also had great nursing and great ICUs. All the components were in place to build a world-class neurosurgical institute.

And it also had the resources. It had great management and a loyal coterie of grateful and generous donors. At the time, Cedars was one of the few medical centers that was not losing money. Even though it functioned as a nonprofit hospital, some of the financial gain from neurosurgery could be made available to finance our translational research, and all of it would not have to be used to offset losses in other departments.

Tom Priselac and I met for dinner. I told him that I was interested in moving over to Cedars-Sinai and what my vision was—to create a brain tumor center of excellence. I handed him my Manhattan Project proposal. He put it to one side, but replied immediately. "I'll read it eventually," he said, "but I'm very much interested in moving forward."

Several days later, I met with Tom Zenty, Cedars's chief operating officer, in his office. He was a tall man, about six-four, and a truly dynamic individual. Today he is president of the entire university hospital system in Cleveland. He'd read my proposal, and we discussed how I saw the brain tumor center developing, and what I thought its potential was in the long term. Then he looked me right in the eye and said, "This is a really nice proposal, Dr. Black, but . . ."

But . . . ? I held my breath briefly, wondering what was coming next.

"But tell me . . . what would it take to build an entire neurosurgical institute?"

In spite of myself, I felt a grin creep across my face.

Several months later, after a series of planning meetings, my move to Cedars-Sinai and the creation of the Maxine Dunitz Neurosurgical Institute was announced.

Before I arrived, Cedars had been doing only twenty-five brain tumor surgeries a year. We are now handling three thousand neurosurgical cases annually, and our staff has grown to more than a hundred. Today we are one of the largest neurosurgical centers in the nation, which helps fund our research efforts. And we have continued our pursuit of the "odd observation."

We built the program at Cedars for guys like Glenn Rhoades, who would soon be receiving several doses of dendritic vaccine to augment the chemotherapy and radiation therapy he'd received after his second surgery. Made with the body's own dendritic cells, this new vaccine is an example of how translational bench-to-bedside research is being deployed to benefit patients. It is as close as we have been able to come thus far to the Anti-Tumor Juice we dreamed about when I was still at the University of Michigan. Combining the dendritic cell vaccine with other therapies, we have managed to bring the two-year survival rate for glioblastoma patients from a mere 8 percent to 42 percent.

Dendritic cells are a key part of our immune system, and were first described in the late nineteenth century by German pathologist Paul Langerhans (who also discovered the Islets of Langerhans, the pancreatic cells that produce insulin). They are the immune system's most effective "presenting" cells for things in our body that need to be attacked and eliminated. Dendritic cells seek out the enemy—bacteria, viruses, or in Glenn's case, anaplastic astrocytoma cancer cells. They then ingest the identifying proteins from the surfaces of these bad cells, process the proteins in a special way, and show them off or "present" them on their own surfaces to the body's killer T-cells.

Killer T-cells are a special variety of white blood cells, or lymphocytes. When the dendritic cells present these bad proteins, they essentially give the killer T-cells the scent, so to speak, so they know what to attack. The killer T-cells then function as a highly efficient assassination squad, destroying the cancer cells that have invaded the brain. The preparation of the vaccine itself involves filtering out the dendritic cells from the patient's blood, growing them in the lab, and then exposing them to the patient's tumor cells that we obtained during surgery.

Six months after his surgery, a smiling Glenn Rhoades sat in the treatment room at the Neurosurgical Institute at Cedars-Sinai, far from the smog-filled days of his childhood, his shirt already off, waiting for his first injection of Anti-Tumor Juice. We were hopeful that the dendritic cell vaccine would complete the job that the surgery, chemotherapy, and radiation probably had not, or at least keep the remaining enemy cells at bay long enough for us to come up with the next generation of ATJ. For Glenn, this was a big moment in the ongoing treatment of his brain tumor, one that he had looked forward to with anxious anticipation for some time.

Glenn would be receiving four vaccine injections in all, followed by regular MRI scans to check for any tumor regrowth. Hopefully there would be none. His most recent MRI had been absolutely clear.

Glenn Rhoades was about to receive a highly targeted brain cancer vaccine to fire up his immune system to go after and eradicate his remaining cancer cells. A week earlier, I had visited Dr. Chris Wheeler, our immunologist who heads up the dendritic vaccine trials, to make sure all was ready. "Do we have enough cells?" I asked.

"We're good," he replied.

"Basically," I started explaining to Glenn, "we stop the chemotherapy before we give the vaccine so . . ."

". . . so it doesn't kill the dendritic cells," he said, flashing a smile as he finished my thought.

"Right," I said, smiling back.

"And so Glenn doesn't get nauseous," he added, his smile broadening.

"Right again."

It was good to see that his sense of humor was intact, but I could have guessed as much from his singular attire. Today, the amateur racecar driver was sporting a Harley-Davidson skullcap, which he usually wore under his motorcycle helmet. A few wisps of his radiation-thinned red hair were peeking out at the sides, adding a whimsical effect. Glenn was ready for his first injection of the vaccine. A milky brew of ten million dendritic cells would be injected just under the skin of his armpit, affording the dendritic cells direct access to the lymph nodes there. Then they would spread out into the rest of his lymphatic system, where they would go to work recruiting millions of killer T-cells to mount an all-out attack against his remaining cancer cells.

"So, how have you been feeling?" I asked.

"I feel great," he answered.

"No seizures?"

"Nothing at all. Any chance I can get off the Keppra, the anti-seizure medication?"

"Not if you're still driving your racecar. Unlike people who might experience a seizure at home or at work, if you have a seizure behind the wheel, you might injure not only yourself but others as well."

"Understood," he said. "Meanwhile, though, I've also been riding my motorcycle and traveling. Carol and I just got back from two weeks in Europe. We were pretty much able to outpace the young people up the stairs at the Eiffel Tower."

"Excellent," I said.

"What are the possible adverse reactions to the vaccine?" he inquired, getting down to business.

"Maybe some swelling and redness," I replied. "We'll keep an eye on you for a couple of hours after the shot, but after treating nearly a hundred patients, we haven't observed any significant adverse reactions. Everything we're giving you is from your own body. Chiayi should be here soon to give you the vaccine."

"I'm ready," he said with a smile.

Chiayi Chen entered the treatment room. She is one of three special research nurses who administer the clinical trials under my direction, taking care of patient scheduling, and collecting various data—patient temperature, blood pressure—and recording and reporting any side effects from the treatment. There is also a great deal of paperwork involved in documenting that proper study protocols are being followed.

"Would you care for Benadryl or Tylenol with your injection?" Nurse Chen asked.

Glenn declined. "I always pass on medications," he said.

After several more questions, and after she had taken his vitals, Nurse Chen asked the big question, which had to be asked quite formally. The dendritic vaccine treatment is experimental, and the permission from the patient to administer it must be absolutely unequivocal.

"Mr. Rhoades, do you wish to continue with the vaccination?" she inquired.

"Yes I do," he answered, raising his left arm to expose the target area.

The moment had arrived. Chiayi Chen took a slight breath and carefully injected ten million of Glenn Rhoades's own dendritic cells into his armpit. The whole procedure was over in thirty seconds, leaving only a small weal where the dendritic cells congregated before making their way into the nearby lymph nodes. Two hours later, with the Anti-Tumor Juice making its way through his lymphatic system, Glenn Rhoades was in his car, making his own way back home to Carlsbad. With luck, he'd beat the worst of the afternoon traffic on the I-5.

The truth is that if the war against the malignant brain tumor is going to be won for patients like Glenn Rhoades, inventing ever more clever ways of cutting out tumors is never going to be enough. It is the new biological therapies that are smarter than the cancer that will be the most effective, therapies like the dendritic vaccine that will hunt down and kill renegade cancer cells that are beyond the reach of the scalpel. And that means that the war on brain tumors is not going to be won in the OR, but rather in the research lab.

We need a more intelligent strategy if we are to be the victors in this war. It is for this reason that a few neurosurgeons, including myself, have been devoting large amounts of our time and resources to research in the lab, to better understand the nature of cancer. We need to learn what it needs to survive, and above all to figure out where it is vulnerable. Only in that way can we develop novel approaches that will ultimately only kill the malignant cells and leave the good brain cells intact.

Neurosurgeons all over the country are starting to "think like a tumor" in order to outsmart it. At Harvard University, neurosurgeon Bob Martuza has been working with a herpes virus to deliver genes to tumor cells that will cause these cells to self-destruct. At Johns Hopkins University, neurosurgeon Henry Brem has developed Gliadel wafers, which are implanted directly into the tumor cavity during surgery to deliver a continuous payload of chemotherapy to kill off remaining cancer cells. And at the National Institutes of Health, neurosurgeon Ed Oldfield has become known for his work in convection-enhanced delivery, where chemotherapeutic drugs are delivered through a catheter down a pressure gradient behind the blood-brain barrier directly into malignant tumors.

After completing my research into the ability of leukotrienes to open the blood-brain barrier, I began looking for other compounds that might do the same thing. It turned out that bradykinin, a naturally occurring protein in the body, also had a potent effect on the blood-brain barrier, and a bradykinin-like drug was developed that we took into clinical trials in brain tumor patients, and patients' lives were extended. Recently, I found that the erectile dysfunction drugs Viagra and Levitra are even more effective in opening the blood-brain barrier than bradykinin. We have now begun clinical studies in patients using Levitra to enable chemotherapeutic drugs to cross the blood-brain barrier into brain tumors. We have shown that we can open these capillaries selectively in the brain tumor to increase delivery of chemotherapy by three- or four-fold. Today, patients whose tumors would have been difficult to reach with chemotherapeutic drugs ten years ago are now taking Levitra, and are getting the benefits of highly focused doses of chemotherapy to their malignant brain tumors without damage to their normal brain tissues.

None of these strategies has yet proven to be the definitive weapon against the malignant brain tumor, but each has been a step in the right direction. In the end, it will be the science, not the scalpel, that wins the war against this vexing adversary.

I began the program at Cedars to win this war, and I take it very personally. It is an unconventional war against a very smart enemy that fights like a terrorist organization, with multiple cells. Cut out one cell, and another cell develops and continues to attack your vital infrastructure. We are constantly working to develop new smart weapons in our war against cancer. Someday we'll get that perfect Anti-Tumor Juice concoction that will win this war for us.

In the meantime, we're advancing on the enemy on all

fronts, taking care of one patient at a time and trying to learn something from each battle we fight. I know we'll get there. The opportunity for breakthroughs and for creating cures has never been greater than it is now. But if cancer is indeed a terrorist, then glioblastoma multiforme, or GBM, is Osama bin Laden. I have lost a dear friend to glioblastoma, and as we catch up once again with William Tao, he is just out of surgery.

CHAPTER 6

Fighting the Terrorist

"How are you feeling today?" I asked Mr. Tao as Suzane and I entered his hospital room. It was late in the afternoon on the day after his surgery.

"Good," he answered from his bed. His tone was certain, but subdued.

Once again, his family stood as we entered. Aside from the slightly askew cap bandage concealing his stitches—his salt-and-pepper hair peeking out at the sides—Mr. Tao looked good—a bit groggy perhaps, but clearly recovering.

"How is your headache, on a scale of one to ten?" I asked him. I enunciated slowly and distinctly, and spoke in somewhat louder tones than I usually do. It was exactly the way you talk when you have a bad long-distance connection—which wasn't far from the truth. There is a persistent fog of anesthesia that hangs over patients the day after surgery, and it takes a concerted effort to penetrate it.

"About three," he answered.

"Good," I said. "Your recovery is right on schedule. Your functions are high and your MRI after surgery looks good—we've gotten everything out that we can see. As I said to you last night, we know there are still microscopic cells remaining, and we'll deal with these with the other therapies we've been talking about."

I had also explained his biopsy results to him last night, while he was still in the ICU. He was not surprised; he had been expecting the worst, he confessed. When I told him that his tumor was a glioblastoma, he had taken the news bravely, and reiterated his resolve to fight the cancer.

"So, Mr. Tao, we've accomplished what we set out to do, at least this far. We'll have the nurses get you up and walking around a little later today. Then maybe you can have a little dinner. Today is Wednesday. So maybe Friday you can go home."

"Very good!" he exclaimed, the lights kindling in his eyes. His family, in attendance around their patriarch as usual, shared his delight at the prospect of his return home.

"I will see you Wednesday for your post-operative exam. And we're going to schedule you to see the radiation therapy doctor and also Dr. Drazin, an oncologist, who will start you on your chemotherapy medicine. On Wednesday when we see you we'll take your stitches out, and talk about the final pathology and the recommendations from the Tumor Board."

Mr. Tao's face darkened briefly at the mention of his treatment, but I could already discern in his demeanor the determination I see in most patients diagnosed with GBMs. The grit that had made Mr. Tao a successful international entrepreneur would serve him well as he fought his tumor.

As Suzane and I bid the Taos good night and turned to leave, his sister took me aside. "He had a lot of fear before," she said in softened tones. "He feels much better now, more confident. Thank you."

"He looks perfect," I answered. "We've got quite some distance to go, but we're off to an excellent start." I had chosen my words carefully. In difficult cases like Mr. Tao's, where the long-term prognosis is undeniably grim, I am always mindful not to promise too much.

What makes the glioblastoma such a formidable enemy is its ability to become invisible to the immune system. Like a terrorist hiding among the everyday population, it masks its identifying "bad" proteins on its surface, so that the immune system cannot recognize it as a cancer. In this sense, the GBM is able to cloak itself like a *Star Trek* Klingon warship, and thereby progress unchallenged by the immune system. When threatened by chemotherapy, it turns on multiple drug-resistant genes that enable it to literally pump the chemotherapy drugs right back out of its cells. The more chemotherapy we infuse into a tumor, the more multiple drug-resistant genes it switches on. Of course, the blood-brain barrier protects brain tumors against most chemotherapy in the first place.

We are constantly making advances against this terrible adversary; new weapons include cancer drugs that target specific pathways in cancer cells, and dendritic vaccines like the one we administered to Glenn Rhoades. Nevertheless, the glioblastoma multiforme continues to earn its brutal reputation. It acts more like a terrorist organization than a biological adversary—constantly changing and constantly shifting its guerrilla strategies. In response, we constantly adjust our own attacks, striving to outsmart the tumor, pushing back the survival frontier, winning for the patient whatever time we can.

Several months later, an exuberant William Tao returned to the clinic for his scheduled exam and MRI. He had just completed his radiation treatments, and was nearing the end of his first round of chemotherapy. His salt-and-pepper hair had been freshly cut and his hair was parted to expose his incision, which was healing nicely. "I do this for you, Dr. Black," he said, smiling as he pointed to his parted hair. "When I go home, I part here instead!"

Mr. Tao was ablaze with positive energy. To his great delight, our oncologist, Dr. Noam Drazin, had dubbed him "Superman." "Dr. Drazin say, 'You are Superman!'" he exclaimed, sitting upright in his chair and throwing his arms over his head in his characteristic "touchdown" sign of victory. "I asked, 'What do you mean?'" he continued. "Dr. Drazin said some patients, their face becomes pale from the radiation—radiation is very strong. Some people have problems, reaction. He said, 'You look very good, so you are

Superman.' He gave me certificate. I say, 'Okay, what is Superman doing in hospital? Superman is not supposed to be in hospital!' "

His family was amused by his retelling of the anecdote, and I could see that making people laugh was something that William Tao very much enjoyed doing. Prior to becoming a real estate magnate, he had appeared in more than thirty Hong Kong films as a comedic actor. Now, even though the gravity of his situation had not changed, his indomitable spirit and his gift for telling colorful stories had reasserted themselves with great vigor.

"He's even more colorful when he's speaking in Chinese," his son Andrew assured me.

I didn't doubt it for a moment. Apart from a rash on the left side of his head, William Tao did look good. The rash was confined to an area just above his eye, and was the result of a shingles attack. One of the unintended consequences of chemotherapy is that it can weaken the immune system, opening the door to viral infections like shingles.

"So, how have you been doing?" I asked. "How have you been spending your days?"

"Waiting to see you!" he said brightly.

I smiled and sat down next to him.

"Well," I said, "I just looked at your MRI scan, and it looks very good."

"Oh, my God! My God!" Mr. Tao shouted, his face ecstatic with relief. He looked like a rocket about to take off, but managed with great difficulty to remain planted in his chair.

"During his treatments, he would say that God was helping him," Andrew said. "He said he never used to believe in God, but recently he is appreciating him."

"Well," I said, "there's no sign of the tumor coming back. We have a really excellent response the way everything is looking. There is no growth, no tumor that we can see on the scan. Everything is perfect."

"You say perfect? Perfect?? Is perfect!??" he asked.

"How are you feeling?" I asked.

"Happy, very happy!" he replied.

Mr. Tao then added something in Chinese, which Andrew translated for him. "My father says that if you want to know his inside feelings, he feels like he's been sent to the keeper of the gates and been turned back by someone who says, 'It's not your time yet.' He feels like he's one of five guys who were sentenced to death by a firing squad . . . all five were lined up against the wall and shot at, and he turned out to be the only survivor."

It was one of the more colorful elaborations on the term "dodging a bullet" I could recall. "Are you having any problems, aside from the shingles?" I asked. "Are you feeling dizzy at times? Any headaches?"

"No," he said, settling down. "Everything is good!"

The radiation treatments had gone well, helping kill the residual tumor cells that surgery had left behind. The chemotherapy agent Temodar, in combination with Levitra, also appeared to be working, preventing the regrowth of Mr. Tao's glioblastoma—for now.

"Okay," he continued. "I have question."

"What is it?"

"Chinese New Year is coming soon. So today I ask you, can I go on a short trip?"

"Yes."

"I thought maybe go to Vegas."

"Go to Vegas." I was aware that Mr. Tao had a well-deserved reputation as a high-roller.

"Vegas is very dangerous," he said with a mischievous twinkle, "but I hope to win some money for your research."

"Thank you," I said. "We can use it."

"Another question," Mr. Tao said. "When can I go back to Hong Kong?"

"He wants to return to Hong Kong for at least two or three months," Andrew added.

"Not right away," I replied. "We're going to need you here until you've finished the vaccine treatment, if you agree to be a part of the study. After you get all the treatments, you can go back."

"What about nutrition?" his son asked. "Should he be eating foods with antioxidants?"

"Eat what you like," I said to Mr. Tao, "but try to eat healthy. It is best to avoid foods with a lot of preservatives, because your body has to detoxify those preservatives. That's more work for your system. As long as you're eating healthy with no preservatives, it's better. But there's no special food you need to eat."

"Can he eat the Chinese medicine soup?" Mrs. Tao asked.

"What is in the medicine soup?" I asked.

"Herbal nutrition," said Andrew.

That didn't give me much to go on. "I'd rather you take just a multivitamin for right now," I replied. "Whatever is in there might counteract the medicine we are giving you. Once you start on the vaccine, you can have the herbal nutrition."

"And what about the maitake mushrooms?" his sister asked. Maitake mushrooms have antioxidant properties, and many cancer patients believe them to be helpful.

"We talked about maitake mushrooms before, and I haven't forgotten about them," I replied. "They would be a good supplement when you get on the vaccine therapy, but not yet.

"I would like to add another drug to your regimen," I continued. "Your tumor looks to be responsive to the Temodar and the Levitra, which is good, but we may be able to get additional benefit if we add Avastin. This is a new drug. It prevents the tumor from growing new blood vessels, starving it of its blood supply. The FDA has approved the use of Avastin in other parts of the body to treat cancer, but it is not yet approved for treatment of brain tumors. Nevertheless, it has been showing some early promise in clinical studies for use with glioblastomas. It may be the most effective medicine we've seen so far for this type of tumor."

"Are there side effects?" Mr. Tao's sister asked.

"There have been few side effects reported with Avastin."

"Few side effects?" he said. "Good!"

"The major risk is bleeding in the brain or tumor, but the risk is small. We want to continue you on that for a few months, and then we'll consider you for the vaccine study, if you agree, probably in about two months."

Avastin (bevacizumab) has been much in the news lately. Unfortunately, most of the press coverage has had little to do with its effectiveness. Avastin is the Maserati of cancer drugs. For breast cancer patients, it may prolong life by several months—at a cost of $100,000 per year. For brain tumors, the annual cost might be twice that, $200,000. Because Avastin does not yet have FDA approval for use with brain cancer, many insurance companies will not pay for it, despite our aggressive appeals that they provide it for our patients. Mr. Tao had a luxury few other individuals did—to be able to make the choice to take it—whether his insurance paid for it or not.

I often talk about risk-benefit analysis in weighing various treatment options for my patients, but when *risk*-benefit analysis turns into *cost*-benefit analysis, it makes me exceedingly uncomfortable. This, I think, is one of the real tragedies of managed care. Let us take a look at one valuable tool in fighting cancer, Gliadel wafers.

These are small biodegradable chemotherapy wafers that we often leave behind in the surgical cavity when a malignant tumor is removed. About the size of a dime, they have a leg up on effectiveness in that they are already beyond the blood-brain barrier. As they dissolve, they release chemotherapy, killing off some of the cancer cells that surgery inevitably left behind. I had considered using them with Mr. Tao, but because we had exposed so many blood vessels around the brain stem, the presence of the wafers posed a significant risk of a brain-stem stroke. Consequently I elected not to use them.

When I chose not to put Gliadel wafers into Mr. Tao's brain cavity, this was clearly a health-based risk-benefit decision. I was concerned about the potential for brain-stem stroke. The wafers cost about $1,000 apiece; traditionally, we put in eight of them. The $8,000 cost was clearly within Mr. Tao's ability to pay. Not long ago there was an excellent double-blind study of the placement of Gliadel wafers in patients diagnosed with malignant astrocytomas—the same kind of cancer that Glenn Rhoades has. A total of 110 of these patients received Gliadel wafers after surgery; 112 patients received placebo wafers without chemotherapy, and no patient knew who got what.

What the study showed was that with Gliadel wafers in the brain, survival was extended by eight weeks. The mean survival for these patients was four months, so that instead of surviving for four months, the patients survived for six. That is a statistically significant increase in survival, but initially a lot of insurance companies refused to pay for the wafers. Medicare itself denied payment until 2007. It doesn't take much to do the math and figure out that at least at the outset, insurance carriers and Medicare had reached the conclusion that two months of life was not worth even $8,000. From their perspective, at those prices, an additional eight weeks did not pencil out.

This is an unfortunate example of what can happen when risk-benefit turns into cost-benefit, but the problem is far larger than any question about the value of the Gliadel wafers themselves. These cold-blooded calculations happen over and over with any number of medicines and treatments, especially those that improve the quality of life for cancer patients without necessarily increasing their survival. Reducing the issue to one of mathematics is appalling, but it is not uncommon. How much is an additional six months of quality life worth? How much is an additional year worth? Is it worth $5,000? $25,000?? $50,000??? And to whom? Who gets to decide? Health care professionals? The patients themselves? Accountants in insurance companies?

I believe it is wrong to let choices in health care be dictated by some sort of value that is arbitrarily assigned to human life—above all by those who have no personal stake in the outcome. Once society attempts to do that, the slope gets slippery very quickly. It is not acceptable to say it's okay for us to spend $200,000 to extend this man's life for a year, but this other guy is worth only $2,000.

And what about those times when the dreadful mathematical calculation turns out to be wrong? You have already met Scott Erdman, who defied the odds, but there are many others.

"Even with Avastin, I still need vaccine?" Mr. Tao asked.

"Mr. Tao," I said, looking directly at him, "you have a very aggressive tumor. It's a very tough fighter. We know that the surgery, the radiation, and the chemotherapy you have already received are not enough to defeat it. We have to continue to give you very strong treatments to make sure we knock it down and kill it. The medicine is a lot. It's a lot to take. But it's very, very important. If we ever let up—even just a little bit, even just a little while—the tumor will have a chance to take hold again and begin to regrow."

"Okay," Mr. Tao said. "No more questions. I will follow you."

"Mr. Tao, we will fight this together," I said. "You're going to get a nice interval here, once you get on the vaccine. It will build up your immune system. It has almost no side effects, and you'll be off chemotherapy. Then in about eight months or so, we'll restart you on chemotherapy, on the Temodar. After the vaccine, the tumor will be even more sensitive to the Temodar. It will be kind of a 1-2-3 punch."

"Okay. Dr. Black, you make decision," Mr. Tao said. "My life is given to you. Happy New Year."

"Happy New Year to you," I answered.

As the Taos exited the room, Mrs. Tao turned to me in the hall and said, "Good news for him today, yes?"

"Yes," I said. "Good news."

There was no way to tell how long the good news would last. Mr. Tao was in a battle for his life, and the odds were against him. Even with his excellent response to radiation and chemotherapy, and the prospect of his participation in the dendritic vaccine trial, his days were probably limited. A year? Maybe two? Perhaps three? It was hard to say.

William Tao is a wealthy man, and who lives and who dies in the medical world too often is dictated by economics—cost-benefit, not risk-benefit. It happens much too frequently that people who can pay get one kind of health care; people who can't get another. The balance between expensive procedures and impoverished patients is frequently decided in cost-benefit pass-the-buck tussles among health insurers and Medicaid or Medicare bureaucrats. For my next patient, this tussle could have cost her her life.

CHAPTER 7

The Doctor's Dilemma

My post-surgery report detonated a major outbreak of jubilation. Elishadie Tezera's large extended family began vigorously hugging one another—and me—to celebrate the good news. I left them to their happiness, and Geno Hunt and I had a brief exchange about what it all meant. The two of us had just spent eight hours in surgery, knowing, number 1, that the hospital was going to lose money; and number 2, that we were going to expose ourselves to the risk of malpractice in case something went wrong and her family decided to sue.

"So . . ." I began, "why did we do that?"

"Because it was just the right thing to do," Geno said simply. "It's not always about the money, is it? We've got to do these things."

"That's what we're here for," I replied. Geno looked at it the same way I did: It absolutely was not always about the money. That was what my father had taught me through word and deed, every day as I was growing up. His passion was for teaching, but he taught me to focus on what was important.

Elishadie Tezera is a young college student from Ethiopia who epitomizes the problem of what happens when poor people get expensive diseases. Elishadie had a brain tumor, an acoustic neuroma, which is a benign tumor that originates in the cells that insulate the balance and hearing nerves as they leave the brain stem on their way to the inner ear. Tumors like this one are a good example of why the terms "benign" and "malignant" are not always useful. Elishadie's acoustic neuroma was termed "benign" because there was no risk that it would spread to other areas of the brain. Nevertheless, as it continued to grow and to press on the brain stem, it would be every bit as deadly as the most aggressive glioblastoma multiforme. The tumor had to come out, but there was only one problem: Elishadie Tezera had no medical insurance.

Tumors have no respect for nationality or the size of your bank account. Given the shortage of neurosurgeons who specialize in brain tumors, the growing number of brain tumors, and the growing number of people who have no health insurance, where can these patients go? This is a tough question, particularly with the more difficult tumors, and it is one that I am forced to wrestle with much more often than I would like. Beyond the dilemmas of whether or not to perform an operation because of the medical risks or potential physical deficits, as a doctor I must also deal with larger, more complicated dilemmas that surround money—not necessarily health.

When Elishadie first arrived at the Cedars emergency room, one of my colleagues, Dr. John Yu, who is the director of our Brain Tumor Center of Excellence, was the neurosurgeon on call. He performed an emergency operation to install a cerebral shunt, relieving the pressure that was building in her brain due to excess cerebrospinal fluid. He saved her life. The next morning, her concerned family asked me to get involved in the case.

At that point, Cedars had already done what we are legally required to do for someone who comes to our ER with a condition that requires immediate medical intervention. For Elishadie, this meant performing the emergency lifesaving installation of the shunt, and stabilizing her before sending her home. Cedars-Sinai Medical Center has an emergency room, but it is not a public hospital. To be admitted here for nonemergent care, patients must be insured, either through a private health insurance plan or through Medi-Cal, which is the California Medicaid program administered by the state Department of Health Services. Patients who have no insurance, unless it is a true life-or-death emergency, are typically not admitted. After Elishadie had been discharged, we asked the social workers to try to get her insured through Medi-Cal. Once the paperwork had been processed and she was covered, we told the family to bring her back so we could remove the tumor as an elective procedure.

I knew we were in a race for time. The Medi-Cal application process is glacially slow, and there is no way to fast-track individual cases based on the urgency of their condition. It would take Elishadie as much as three to four months to qualify for insurance, but looking at the CT and the MRI, I was pretty sure that she couldn't wait that long. The shunt had relieved the pressure for the moment, but it was only a stopgap measure. The tumor was still growing. It was probably only a matter of weeks before the pressure on her cranial nerves and brain stem would bring on a new wave of symptoms. Elishadie would continue to deteriorate, and to lose function. Ultimately the pressure would send her into a coma; death would follow. Before she got coverage, she could have died of red tape.

To be sure, a tumor operation at Cedars-Sinai was not her only option. Every patient in this country has health care. Not every patient is insured, but every patient has health care. It would have been fairly straightforward for me to refuse to do the surgery. Had I done that, I would have referred her to one of several large public hospitals in the area, where they would remove the tumor.

And this was my doctor's dilemma: Do I send Elishadie to the county hospital? Do I turn this lovely girl away, a young woman whose family is begging me to do the surgery and to take care of her, to make sure that she has the best chance? Before I made the referral, I would have to ask myself the question I always ask: Is this in the best interest of the patient? In my heart of hearts, do I really believe that she will have the best chance of having a good outcome if the surgery is done at a county hospital rather than here?

And in Elishadie's case, when I was honest with myself, that answer had to be no. I'd already done that once before, with heartbreaking results. A few years earlier, I had referred an older woman to a county facility. Like Elishadie, she was foreign-born, in that case from Belize. Like Elishadie, she had an acoustic neuroma at the brain stem. And also like Elishadie, she was uninsured. When I made the referral, I told her family to ask specifically and by name for an experienced senior neurosurgeon there, a man who I knew to be quite competent. I was confident that she would have a good outcome, and I called the doctor the day after the operation to see how she was doing. Unbeknownst to me, he had not performed the surgery, and a junior attending surgeon, unskilled in tumors, had been assigned to her case. Right after she came out of surgery, she had a major hemorrhage. She never regained consciousness. She was dead. Needless to say, the family was devastated. Even though I was not directly responsible for what happened, I felt dreadful nevertheless.

The last thing I wanted was to repeat that tragedy. Elishadie was just slightly older than my own daughter, Teal, and she was taking pre-med courses in college, hoping to become a doctor. Those factors tugged at me, but even putting past history and emotion aside, when I looked at the case clinically from a risk-benefit perspective, the arguments were compelling. It would be a challenging surgery, but I'd done many like it before. I was highly confident that I could remove the acoustic neuroma entirely. The tumor was fully encapsulated. Once it was out, it would not grow back. This was not a matter of buying time; Elishadie would be cured, with no neurological deficits. She would have her entire life ahead of her. I could not say with any certainty that the outcome would be that positive if I sent her elsewhere.

For this patient, the risk-benefit analysis weighed heavily in favor of doing the surgery here at Cedars—the question was whether we would beat the clock. When we discharged Elishadie after installing the shunt, we gave her steroids to help control the swelling. We also told her that if her condition started to deteriorate before her Medi-Cal coverage came through, she should phone me and then head back to the Cedars ER.

About a month after getting the shunt, that's exactly what happened. Elishadie called me to say she was going downhill. As we had discussed, she came again to our ER. The acoustic neuroma was now pressing on her seventh cranial nerve, creating facial weakness. It was also pushing on the eighth cranial nerve, making her deaf in her left ear and affecting her balance. The tumor was relentlessly compressing her brain stem, which contains the hardwiring for critical body functions, such as consciousness, movement, and sensation. Elishadie was becoming increasingly weak. The increasing pressure from the tumor was on the brink of creating irreversible neurological damage to delicate structures within the brain—before sending her into the coma that would precede her death.

Because she had gotten worse, the rules of the game had changed. Elishadie was once again in a potentially life-threatening situation. Given her symptoms, at that point we as a hospital had to step up. Putting in the shunt was no longer the required lifesaving intervention; removing the tumor was. It had ceased to be an elective surgery—it had become what we had to do to prevent her death. I fully documented her deteriorating condition, admitted her, bulldozed a spot for her on my surgical schedule the next day, and made a mental note that Accounting would just have to take the hit. Elishadie was out of time, and bringing her in through the ER was the only way I could make it work.

Her surgery was going to be an arduous eight-hour trek into deepest Tiger Country. Geno worked with me on the operation. He did the opening, removing a round section of Elishadie's skull and reflecting back the dura mater. Before I began, I asked the OR tech to rotate Elishadie's body slightly to give me better access to the surgical opening just behind her left ear. I called for the scope and brought the lights down in the OR.

We faced a significant hurdle right at the beginning. One of the early dangers in this operation was that the cerebellum could swell up at us. Located at the back and bottom of the brain, the cerebellum, or "little brain," oversees the regulation and coordination of movement, posture, and balance.

Swelling of the cerebellum was a threat because of the buildup of intracranial pressure. The MRI scan had revealed that the large schwannoma, which was about the size of a peach, was obstructing the fourth ventricle, and was causing the accumulation of fluid. If there was enough fluid and enough pressure to cause the cerebellum to swell, it would obstruct our access to the tumor. We had to make sure the cerebellum was relaxed—without forcibly retracting it.

As a rule I do not retract healthy brain tissue, because it is difficult to do so without creating neurological deficits. Retracting goes against one of the fundamental operating tenets essential to being a thief in the night in the OR: In surgery, the only part of the brain that should ever know I was there is the tumor. In Elishadie's case, I did not want to risk injury to her cerebellum, but we had to make sure it stayed out of the way. We gently supported it as we drained off some spinal fluid. Once we did, the cerebellum just naturally relaxed.

In removing the tumor there were several important landmarks in Tiger Country that had to be treated with the utmost care. I had to be careful working around the facial nerve—the seventh cranial nerve. If I damaged it, Elishadie would never move one side of her face or smile again. I worked my way along it, peeling the tumor away. Progress was painstakingly slow and laborious. Above all,

I had to peel the tumor away from the brain stem without damaging it. The brain stem contains the wiring for the entire neurological circuitry of the body. It is the arousal center for alertness. If it gets damaged even slightly, the results are profound. One wrong move around the brain stem—the slightest bruising—could result in a devastating brain-stem stroke or coma—which is what had happened to the unfortunate woman from Belize.

The only thing separating the tumor from the brain stem was a double thickness of arachnoid tissue—very, very thin, transparent onionskin membrane. One layer belonged to the tumor, and the other belonged to the brain stem. They adhered, one to the other, and my job was to go in on the plane between them and separate them, virtually cell by cell, to tease the tumor away from the brain stem.

It took much of the day, but by 3 p.m., I sent off the tumor samples to pathology and asked Geno to do the closing. It was time to go talk to the family—all of them. Her parents were not present, but a sizeable contingent of apprehensive aunts, uncles, and cousins milled about in the waiting room, pacing, comforting one another, and anxiously awaiting word of Elishadie's outcome.

"She did fine," I announced to the group. "Dr. Hunt is still closing. Even after she gets out of surgery, however, we'll have to keep her on steroids for a bit, to prevent further swelling. You should know that she will also continue to have headaches for a while, but they will abate. The tumor is gone, and the cranial nerves have been preserved.

Elishadie may have some mild facial weakness when she wakes up, but I expect her to make a complete recovery. By this time tomorrow, we'll have her up and walking the halls."

As soon as these words left my lips, I was all but engulfed in the joyous celebration of Elishadie's family. And it was at that moment when I knew the risk had been worth the reward. It was yet another demonstration that it can't always be about the money.

And indeed, if somehow it really *was* about the money, I had spent my career in the wrong end of the neurosurgery business. If the profit motive is what drives you as a neurosurgeon, you should be working in the spine, not the brain. Financially, a neurosurgeon whose practice is 90 percent spinal work is doing very well. For reasons I do not fathom, private health insurance pays neurosurgeons a lot more for spine surgery than for brain surgery. The way that the codes have been set up, there is a huge disparity in the reimbursement system. Payment for a relatively simple spine operation is greater than for a long and complex brain tumor operation. A neurosurgeon can do a single thirty-minute spine operation and make more money than I would get for doing Elishadie's eight-hour tumor operation—if it had been covered by insurance.

That's just one of many reasons why, as a physician, I prefer being at Cedars. At many hospitals the surgeons function in many respects as if they have a private practice. They receive a fee for every patient they operate on.

More operations equals more money. Regardless of your best intentions, it's hard to keep the crude mathematics of that fact from creeping into your risk-benefit assessment of what is best for the patient.

Here at the Neurosurgical Institute at Cedars-Sinai, we have removed the financial motivation to do surgery. All of our full-time faculty are paid employees of the hospital, which means that we get paid by the hospital, not by each case that we do. I'm on salary; I get paid the same amount whether I do one surgery a year or two hundred. When I look at a patient and make a recommendation, there is no financial gain in it for me one way or the other. I can do what I do at a higher level—it becomes more of a calling, and less of a business.

It makes it much easier for me to do my job. I have to run an institute. The institute has a number of missions it has to support: research, translational work, recruiting the best doctors and nurses in the world, and having the facilities that we need to be outstanding. Obviously, we have to make sure that the institute is not losing money, but at the heart of it all is the sense of duty to take care of people who need help.

Cedars has been incredibly supportive of what I do. I am indeed fortunate to have a formidable group of dedicated fund-raisers in my corner. Maxine Dunitz gave the founding gift for the Neurosurgical Institute. Another group of remarkable women who support our work call themselves the Brain Trust, and they are truly a force of nature. Headed by Pauletta Washington, Keisha Whitaker, Johnnie Cochran's widow, Dale, and several other remarkable women, they have raised more than $20 million for us to date. We couldn't do what we do without them.

We take care of people. Part of what we are doing is God's work, and what I like about the way it is set up now is that there is no conflict of interest for me. There is no incentive to do surgeries, but there is no incentive to turn people away, either.

I worked on a young Ethiopian boy who was brought to the United States by a relief organization called Save the Children. Elijah was getting headaches and was becoming unresponsive. The local doctor said that he needed a CT scan, but apparently there is only one CT scanner in all of Ethiopia. When he finally got the scan a couple of months later, they found a huge posterior fossa tumor, an ependymoma. This was an aggressive tumor, and no neurosurgeon in the country would operate on him.

The family got in contact with Save the Children, and someone involved with the charity brought the boy's scans to me. This was clearly a charity case, which meant that we would do the surgery pretty much for free. Even though it would be a $100,000 operation, the hospital agreed to do it for $8,000. If the organization could come up with $8,000, Cedars would accept it as payment in full.

Save the Children raised the money and someone bought Elijah a ticket to the United States. He came with his uncle. Unfortunately, they were ticketed only as far as

New York, but the flight attendants on the plane kicked in their frequent-flyer miles to get them the rest of the way. Elijah landed in Los Angeles quite literally with nothing. He did not have a change of clothes, and his uncle had no place to stay.

When I told the Brain Trust about Elijah, they went into action, raising money for clothing and other necessities. It turned out that we had an anesthesiologist on staff who was also from Ethiopia, and his family took the uncle in while Elijah was being treated. We did the surgery, and Elijah did very well. Pauletta and Denzel Washington gave him a nice going-away party at their home, and he left with about three backpacks full of toys and clothes.

There was not a word in the press. Cases like this are not that uncommon; you just never hear about them. Elijah was a special case because he was brought from overseas, but how often can we take care of people like Elishadie Tezera? With the support of the administration and the backing of our strong donors, Cedars underwrote the $50,000 cost of Elishadie Tezera's surgery. I hoped that Elishadie, the aspiring doctor, would pay it forward and go on to save a few lives herself, which will make her surgery all the more worthwhile.

What I did for Elishadie I cannot do for everyone. I am mindful that I cannot provoke a stampede of uninsured neurosurgery patients to our door. It would be irresponsible. Although Cedars-Sinai is a nonprofit hospital, we will always be restricted in our ability to admit uninsured patients, except those who require immediate lifesaving care. That should be apparent—the ever-mounting problems of health insurance are nationwide in scope. I continue to struggle with these issues, but they are beyond my ability to solve, and beyond the ability of Cedars-Sinai to solve.

What does not escape my attention is that at Cedars-Sinai and indeed at any number of large urban hospitals across the country, the patients who are most likely to be impoverished and uninsured are people of color. Whenever I am pushed into making the kind of choice I had to make for Elishadie Tezera, for too often my patient is black, brown, or foreign-born. The playing field in medicine is still far from level—both on the giving end and on the receiving end. As you will see in the next chapter, I had to deal with it, both as a child and as an adult.

CHAPTER 8

Breaking Barriers

"*You* want to be a neurosurgeon?" the chairman asked as I stood before his big oak desk wearing my best suit and tie. I could hear the condescending incredulity in his voice. "What makes you think *you* can be a neurosurgeon?"

He stopped just short of calling me "boy." No one had warned me that the head of the department of neurosurgery at the University of Michigan believed that blacks—and women, for that matter—had no place in neurosurgery, and he would not accept them into "his" program, not as long as he was in charge. The chairman didn't even bother to ask me about my performance in medical school, or about my research achievements. To him they were irrelevant. I had no business being there, and as far as he was concerned, that was the end of it.

As a small child, I had grown up with the overt racism of the South, which was always in-your-face straightforward, right out in the open for all to see. This situation was underhanded, more subtle perhaps, but no less discriminatory. All I knew was that I wanted to become a neurosurgeon, and that here I was, being judged not by my ability but merely by the color of my skin—again.

"You have to be smart to be a neurosurgeon," he continued with the same patronizing tone in his voice. "You have to be able to think on your feet. What do your parents do?"

The year was 1978, and even in the North, there were not yet many African-Americans in the "elite" specializations like neurosurgery and heart surgery. I was still an exception, an anomaly—not just in neurosurgery, not just in medicine, but even in academia at large. A scholarly, highly educated black man may have been unusual, but this was exactly who I had been raised to become. *What did my parents do?* If the chairman knew what my parents, Robert and Lillian Black, had done for my brother and me, and indeed for all the African-American children in Auburn, Alabama, every single day, the question would have died in his throat.

I was brought up to believe that there was nothing that I could not do. My parents saw to it that there were no limits on my imagination, my education, or my ambition. As a child, it never occurred to me that my choice of career would be limited by the color of my skin—although that certainly occurred to others around me. After all, for much of my childhood, George Wallace was the governor of

Alabama—and his wife, Lurleen, was the governor the rest of the time. I was just starting elementary school in 1963, when he blocked the doorway of Foster Auditorium at the University of Alabama to prevent two black students from enrolling—what has since become notorious as the "Stand in the Schoolhouse Door." It took a direct confrontation by federal marshals, led by a future US Attorney General and backed up by the Alabama National Guard, to get Wallace to step aside.

A month earlier, Bull Connor, the commissioner of public safety for the city of Birmingham, had ordered his officers to use fire hoses, cattle prods, and police dogs on civil rights protesters. Television cameras captured the brutality that followed, and showed it to the rest of the world. Race relations had not become violent in our hometown of Auburn, which was a quiet college community built around Auburn University. There was never any doubt, however, that you were in the heart of the Confederacy: A local rock still marks the place where General William Tecumseh Sherman tore up the tracks to cut off the movement of Confederate ammunition.

In 1964, exactly a century after Sherman's March to the Sea and a decade after *Brown v. Board of Education* was handed down by the Supreme Court, the South was still a highly segregated society, and separate was most assuredly not equal. My father, Robert Black, Sr., was a dedicated tactician of the civil rights movement. He was a charter member of Auburn's Biracial Committee, which included ministers, both black and white, several other teachers, and the Auburn University registrar. In Auburn, the mayor and the rest of the white power structure were aware of my father's committee, but made no attempt to harass the group openly, or to try to quash them. It was all very genteel, at least on the surface, but they were surely resistant to change.

My father knew that the status quo would not hold, and he called repeatedly for the community to prepare itself for the inevitable move toward integration and equality. He not only insisted on new textbooks for his students, not hand-me-downs, he also demanded paved roads in black neighborhoods and the integration of the police and fire departments. Nevertheless, there were still places in town that continued to be off-limits to us. One of them was the town's public swimming pool: The "public" didn't include black people.

But even that was about to change. "You don't want those other boys carrying your weight," my father declared to my brother and me at the dinner table one evening in the summer of '64. He was referring to two of his former students, who had jumped into the whites-only pool that afternoon. He didn't exactly say he put them up to it, but he didn't say he didn't, either. A very forward-looking, proactive man, my father had taught his students to engage in civil disobedience. To the consternation of Auburn's mayor, many of them were often seen demonstrating outside City Hall.

Beyond his political activism, he remained at heart an educator. Moreover, his concept of education went far beyond the boundaries of traditional book-learning. Operating within the restrictions of a segregated society, he made it his mission to create the best school system he could for black children, one that would prepare them for the world—not just educationally, but socially and ethically as well. He knew the first names of all 750 of his students, and he required them to dress properly for school. If a boy came to school with his shirttail out, or without a belt, odds were that he would be sent home. The same went for the staff; any male teacher showing up without a tie was shown the door. The dress code applied double to my brother and me. It was important for us to set a good example; there was no way either of us could leave the house without being respectfully attired. My father was a community leader, and his family always had to represent that image.

His regard for proper presentation extended to our home. Our house was small, but he kept both it and the yard immaculate. We lived in a small subdivision in the northeast section of Auburn that had been built to house the town's black professionals, mostly teachers. It was a quiet neighborhood, surrounded by a forest of pine trees—the source of many of my early scientific experiments. The homes along the neighborhood's paved streets were all freshly painted, with neatly trimmed lawns and sewer systems, just like those in Auburn's white neighborhoods.

My father expected nothing less, and nothing less was acceptable to him. During his tenure as principal, he had made Boykin Elementary, in many respects, superior to local white schools. This rubbed some of the whites in the community the wrong way. So did sending my brother to a private boarding school up North. He accepted their ire and the racial animosity that came with promoting excellence among African-Americans with great courage, in part because he came from a long line of family members who had done the same thing.

My father is the proud son, grandson, and great-grandson of Alabama landowners. His great-grandfather Thomas M. Black had come to the United States from Jamaica as a free man, and had made his fortune as a builder in Charleston, South Carolina. In the middle of the nineteenth century he moved his family to Monroe County, Alabama, and historical records show that he was a registered voter there in 1860—*before* the Civil War. He died in 1888 at the age of 109, leaving an estate of 1,080 acres, much of which is still in the family today.

This was the mantle on our shoulders as my brother and I set out for the all-white pool that August afternoon in 1964. Bob was fifteen; I was not quite seven. As we walked out the front door, my father gave us money to buy tickets to the pool. "Don't you jump in without paying," he admonished. Four of Bob's friends came with us: Doris Tolbert, Charles and Bernard Reese, and Cecil Griffin. The mid-afternoon sun was hot; the smell of the asphalt rose up from the road as we made our way down Lincoln Street, then out of the neighborhood, through the outlying black and working-class white neighborhoods, and across town toward the pool. There would be no opportunity to change once we got there, so we all wore our bathing suits under our clothes.

We weren't doing this because of the lack of a place to swim. The year before, my father had talked the town council into building a pool on the campus of all-black Drake High School. It may have been that the city funded it in part out of guilt—two black children had drowned while swimming in the gravel pits, which would fill up with rainwater in the summer. It was never my father's intention, however, for the construction of the blacks-only pool to be an end in itself. At the dedication ceremony, a black minister stood up and said, "Now we ducks can go wading in our own pool!" My father became infuriated. He jumped to his feet and declared, "This is a beginning, not an end. Our youngsters have been going swimming in the gravel pit in their shorts. Now they will know to take a shower and to put on swim trunks before they get into a pool. And that is a prelude to their going into the *next* pool." And with that, he put both the black and white communities in Auburn on notice that he would not be a part of any effort that would perpetuate segregation.

"You sure we're going to be okay?" Doris asked. She was nervous.

"Don't worry," my brother reassured us. "It's all set."

Indeed, the path before us had been carefully prepared. My father would not have sent his children blindly into a dangerous situation. He had floated the idea at a meeting of the Biracial Committee, which he now chaired. What would happen, he posited to the other committee members, if a couple of Negro children—names were not mentioned—were to jump in the white pool? It was a trial balloon, and it had the desired effect. Word got back to the mayor, just as my father knew it would. When no admonition came back from City Hall, he knew the coast was clear.

"C'mon, Keith," Bob said, giving me a light tug as we made our way along Opelika Road to the Perry Street entrance to the pool. We all seemed to be moving to the beat of the same drum. Was it my father's words playing in our young brains? Earlier that week he had said to the committee, "We've been meeting for years. It's time for us to move beyond the coffee-drinking stage. We haven't desegregated one restaurant on College Street. I want Bob Jr. and Keith to be able to go into any restaurant on College Street!"

As we reached the parking lot at the back entrance of the pool, we could hear the voices of the people and the splashing sounds of the children jumping and playing in the water.

"Okay," my brother said, "let's go." We shucked our clothes and, now in our swimming trunks, headed for the fenced gate that led to the pool.

"You kids can't come in here," the gate attendant said

sternly. We held out our money to buy the tickets, but he wouldn't accept it. We just stood there for several minutes, the six of us. Two lifeguards had now joined the man blocking the gate, but we were firm in our resolve. Our standoff was starting to gather attention—a hubbub was brewing. Just then, in the midst of the commotion, several of us—including my brother and me, and Doris Tolbert—managed to slip through the gate. We dashed across the crowded poolside area, past the surprised families and kids, and dove headfirst into the no-longer all-white pool, luxuriating in the feel of the water on our bodies and reveling for a moment in our act of civil disobedience.

It was over relatively fast. None of us expected to spend the afternoon swimming around in the white pool. We jumped in, made our statement, and got out. The police appeared just as we grabbed our clothes. They took down our names, but we didn't get arrested. They just told us we didn't belong there. We all went home, relieved that we weren't going to jail. We'd made our statement. My father had made his. There was no turning back the clock on what we had accomplished that day.

While the Civil Rights Act of 1964 outlawed segregation, discrimination can't simply be legislated out of existence. Because I was so young that summer, there was a lot about racial hostility that I did not yet understand. It wasn't until after we left Auburn and moved to Ohio that I finally understood why we drove the sixteen hours nonstop from Alabama to Michigan whenever we went to visit my aunt in Detroit. My father, my mother, and later my brother shared the driving, while I slept in the back of the Buick. I'd always thought we drove straight through because we were in a hurry to get there, or maybe just to save money. Only later did I find out that it was because we didn't have a choice. The motels along the way wouldn't give us a room for the night—because we were African-American.

It was an indicator that racism did not stop at the Mason-Dixon Line, but there were many others. A main reason for the move to Cleveland was so that I could attend Shaker Heights High School, a secondary school that was part of one of the best public school systems in the country. Before I could enroll there, however, we had to find a home within the boundaries of the school district.

That turned out to be more difficult than we anticipated. In suburban Shaker Heights, as elsewhere, there was an unofficial color line that separated white neighborhoods from black neighborhoods, and every Realtor knew where it was. They called it redlining, and all of them had their sly ways of screening would-be buyers and tenants to ensure that no black families moved into white neighborhoods. Looking for a place to live, we ran into several of them. The last straw was when my parents found a house they really liked and put down first and last month's rent to hold it. The agent took their check, then returned it a day later, saying, sorry, there had been "a mistake"—the house was already rented.

After that, they got in touch with an activist fair housing organization called Human Relations, which provided a white couple who posed as Robert and Lillian Black. They signed a lease on our behalf—it was the only way we were going to get a house in Shaker Heights. The couple even helped us move in. While we were all there together, they invited the landlord over for coffee, so he could see that they'd settled in. Then they introduced my parents as the real Robert and Lillian Black. He was furious. As my mother observed, "I've never seen anybody turn so red."

"My mother would turn over in her grave if she knew I had rented her house to Negroes!" he cried. He called out racial epithets; he even threatened to sue, but legally he was pretty much without recourse. In point of fact, he'd been duped into obeying the law. He did keep a key to the house, and my mother said he would let himself in from time to time to check up on us—she could always tell when he'd been poking around. As it turned out, however, the neighbors were friendly. Shortly after we moved in, the lady next door came over with a pie, and I was enrolled in the Shaker Heights school system that fall.

Even years later at a very progressive institution like the University of Michigan, racial bias persisted. This was almost thirty years ago, and to be sure, things are much different—and much better—today. Back then, however, to get into the residency program in neurosurgery, first I had to get by the chief resident in medicine, whose evaluation could make or break my chances of being admitted.

During the third and fourth years of med school, grading of students becomes very subjective. Your evaluation on a particular rotation is based less on your academic work in the classroom than on what the attending physicians and residents think of you.

At Michigan, their subjective opinion of your presentations and your performance in terms of patient management was crucial—and they knew it. I noticed early on that if you were a white student and said absolutely nothing during the rotation, you would probably be considered a B student. If you were a minority student and kept silent, however, it was more likely that you'd be pegged as a C student. I tried to speak up often, but since performance ratings evaluations are subjective, an evaluator's preconceived notion of how smart you are could significantly influence your grade.

We were making rounds on the second day of my medicine rotation when we stopped by the bedside of a patient with subacute bacterial endocarditis—a disease where bacteria gather on the heart valves. The chief resident was looking into the patient's eyes and I asked, "Did you see any Roth's spots?"

"And what are Roth's spots?" he asked. I knew right away that was not what he meant. There was a disdainful look on his face and distinct edge in his voice when he said it. The message was unmistakable: What he was implying was, "*You* couldn't possibly know what Roth's spots are."

Roth's spots were not something that a medical student at my point in the program would be expected to know about, but ever since my days poring over the *Index Medicus* in high school, I'd continued to read voraciously about different medical conditions. "They are flame-shaped hemorrhages in the retina that are due to the bacteria embolizing through the blood vessels in the retina," I replied.

"They're not flame-shaped," the chief resident said haughtily in his best know-it-all voice. "They're round."

"Here we go again," I said to myself. "It's gonna be one of those." My own personal early warning antennae were twitching furiously.

Thanks to my father, I had developed a heightened internal radar system that alerted me to the impending onset of any racially tinged confrontation. The resident was wrong, but I could not contradict him directly. He was a gatekeeper—if I wanted to get into neurosurgery, I had to get honors in medicine, and this guy was standing between me and my honors for the rotation. He was the chief resident, I was the medical student, and he clearly had the upper hand.

Rather than refute him outright then and there, I decided to save my response for another day. At Michigan, medical students went through a grueling process called Kelly Rounds, which were named after the chairman of the department of medicine, the legendary William Kelly. All of us had to present a patient in front of a large and highly critical audience that included all of the medicine attending physicians, the chief of medicine, the medicine residents and students, and Dr. Kelly himself. Each of us would take our turn in the crosshairs, knowing that we would be grilled mercilessly by the group.

When my turn came up, the patient I was to present suffered from ulcerative colitis. As quickly as I could, I devoured everything I could read about it. I became a walking encyclopedia of ulcerative colitis. Obviously the chief resident was going to be gunning for me, but I decided that I would not live down to his expectations. It was time to stand and deliver.

While an undergraduate, I had taken up the martial art of tai chi. Unlike karate, which opposes force with a stronger force, tai chi teaches us to take a negative force and turn it back on itself. I would do the same thing with the chief resident. I wasn't going to make him look bad—I was going to let him do that all by himself.

In these presentations, you must state what are called "significant negatives." If a symptom or sign is a key indicator in a particular disease, it is clinically important when the patient does not exhibit that symptom or sign. I started off my presentation by saying that Mr. Jones was a forty-two-year-old man who presented with a particular set of symptoms, but not with others.

"That's not important," the chief resident cut in. "That doesn't have anything to do with ulcerative colitis."

"Actually, yes, it does," I replied, handing him a published study confirming what I was saying. "And here are several more copies," I added as I passed them around to the other attendings, and to Dr. Kelly.

I went on, saying that the patient also denied any symptoms of such and such.

"That's not associated with ulcerative colitis," declared the chief resident, interrupting once more.

"Oh, but it is," I answered, passing around another research paper that confirmed what I had said.

The chief resident continued to interrupt, and I continued to hand out papers. He set off each and every one of the booby traps I'd laid for him in my presentation. Not only did I conclude that he was a bigot, he was a slow learner, too.

By the time I had finished, this guy had shrunk down to nothing. There's nothing quite like humiliating yourself in front of your peers. I never had any trouble with him from then on. In fact, he gave me honors on the rotation. Better yet, after that incident my reputation spread, and none of the other chief residents messed with me much, either. As a result of my presentation, I also got an invaluable letter of recommendation for neurosurgery from the chairman of medicine himself, Dr. William Kelly.

Unfortunately racial barriers still exist today, in subtle yet pervasive ways. There are few if any African-Americans who have escaped the sting of prejudicial treatment firsthand. Nevertheless, we must continue to challenge and change minds, even if it's only one mind at a time. While I was a neurosurgery resident at Michigan, a patient returned to see me in the clinic after I had removed his brain tumor. "You know," he said, "I would like to thank you for two things—one, for saving my life, and two, for changing my point of view. Before you took out my brain tumor, I didn't like black people. Perhaps this is a message from God that I should not be a racist anymore."

And what happened to the other bigot? The chairman of the department of neurosurgery? He suffered a series of devastating strokes before I had to face him again and officially apply for a residency in "his" program. Ironically, there was nothing that his own branch of medicine—neurosurgery—could do to repair the damage to his brain. He retired. He was replaced by Dr. Julian T. "Buz" Hoff, one of Michigan's greatest chiefs of neurosurgery, who became one of my most important mentors.

To become a neurosurgeon, I had to make it over a series of barriers that were tougher for me than they were for other students. I never would have made it without the encouragement and assistance of any number of individuals who helped me at key points along the way. From my parents, to the researchers at the University of Pennsylvania who invited me into their lab when I was wandering the halls while my father was in class, to several physicians in the program at the University of Michigan, I have had mentors who wanted me to succeed and who shepherded me through the maze.

I am forever in their debt, and I feel a genuine obligation to help pave the way for the next generation. At Cedars we have created a mentoring program called Brainworks that introduces gifted minority and low-income students to medicine, in particular to neurology and neurosurgery. It's very important for them to understand that they have opportunities—that this could be a future profession for them.

About 1,200 students have come through the program so far—the kids get to be neurosurgeon for a day and to talk with our scientists and surgeons. It's fascinating to me to watch their faces light up as they try on a career in neurosurgery for size. My friend Forest Whitaker calls it "the seed of hope"—an empowering belief in their own possibilities.

It is the same kind of optimistic belief in the future that I try to instill in my patients, no matter how grim their prognosis may be. But I already knew that one of my patients, William Tao, was now really struggling in that regard.

CHAPTER 9

Optimistic Alternatives

I am very good husband!" William Tao called out at the top of his voice. I was still out in the hall, but I heard him clearly. "In Hong Kong everybody knows I am good husband. In home, I cook everything.

"Twenty years I cook. Every day!" he wailed as I walked into the room. The reason he was here today was to draw the white blood cells we needed to make his dendritic vaccine—the Anti-Tumor Juice. It had been almost a year since his surgery, and a few months since his last office visit.

Medically, his news remained good. So far, his MRI scans remained clear of tumor—he was still fighting off the glioblastoma. As his extended family rose to greet me, it was painfully apparent that his entourage, although still sizeable, was missing a couple of members—his wife and her brother were not present. Sometime after the last ecstatic "good news" visit a few months earlier, Mrs. Tao had filed for divorce.

"Superman" now had a broken heart. This unhappiness was not something I had anticipated in his particular case, but these kinds of emotional crises are not uncommon for my patients. Having someone in the family with a brain tumor can be extremely stressful on the family. There is stress for the patient, for the spouse, for the children, and stress for the family as a unit. As physicians we get just tiny glimpses into what goes on behind the closed doors of the family dynamic, but serious illness of any kind tends to bring out any emotional baggage that patients and their families are carrying, and some are hauling more than others.

"Mr. Tao, I know that your divorce is affecting you greatly," I said as gently as I could manage, "but you can't let this get to you."

"Okay, sorry," Mr. Tao said. "Sorry."

"He's very upset," his sister said.

"I can see that," I replied. "But the important thing, Mr. Tao, is that you cannot get stressed."

"Yes, yes. My old friend told me, don't think about this."

From a medical point of view, his broken heart was more than unfortunate. "Stress will hurt your immune system," I told him. "It will hurt the ability of your immune system to fight the cancer. The important thing now is *you*. You must surround yourself with people who care about you and want you to be well, and not worry. This is extremely important for your health."

"Okay. Sorry, sorry."

I've been doing this now for almost a quarter century, and there is no doubt in my mind that the patient's mental and emotional health are strongly connected to physical wellness. It concerns me when one of my patients is depressed or in a state of prolonged anxiety, because emotional state is a powerful contributing factor to survival—either in the positive or in the negative. I have had many patients—Scott Erdman among them—whose sunny outlook, strong support from friends and family, and devout faith in a higher power have played a key role in their survival.

Conversely, numerous studies have shown that relentless stress impairs the immune system. If the brain is depressed, it releases different hormones, different signals in the body, and these affect how we heal from disease. If a patient is being sued or is going through a divorce, these issues may work against the body's ability to fight the tumor. For this reason, I do my best to try to get my patients into a healthy state of mind, where they are eating healthily, sleeping soundly, living well, and surrounded by their loved ones.

Mr. Tao had great affection for his wife, and her abrupt departure pained him greatly. Andrew Tao put his hand on his father's shoulder. "Let's talk about your treatment," he said, hoping to change the subject.

"Okay."

"We're doing very well," I began. "We're coming up to one year from your surgery, and your films look perfect."

"You mean, it's still clear?" Andrew asked, in a voice equal parts astonishment and celebration.

"God bless!" Mr. Tao exclaimed.

"There is no tumor that we can see," I continued. "We're now going to try to go back once more and get you on the vaccine. We don't know why we weren't able to get enough cells."

This would be our second attempt to make dendritic vaccine for him. On the first effort, William Tao had spent a couple of hours hooked up to a blood filtering apparatus that harvested the monocytes—immature white blood cells—that we would need to make the vaccine. It was the same procedure Glenn Rhoades had gone through, but with Mr. Tao, we were unable to get enough monocytes to produce it.

We were puzzled; it was the first time a problem of this sort had occurred. Had his cells simply failed to grow? Was there a problem in the processing of his cultures? It was a major topic of discussion at one of our weekly Tumor Board meetings, and the participants put forth a number of hypotheses from the point of view of their particular specialties. One of our senior research scientists, Gentao Liu, theorized that the problem had to do with the preservative we were keeping the harvested cells in. An infection might have been a contributing factor, thought immunologist Chris Wheeler. Mr. Tao's tumor sample had tested positive for endotoxins—had he developed an infection before surgery, or had something worked its way into the mix afterward, when we were preparing the vaccine? A second tumor sample tested negative for endotoxins.

"Today we're going to try again," I said. "We hope everything will work this time."

"Okay."

"We have one patient taking the vaccine who has been alive now for over nine years, and we've been doing this for ten years. We care a lot about you, but it's very important for you not to grieve about your divorce."

"Okay. One more question . . ." he began, then stopped and reverted to speaking Chinese.

Andrew translated for him. "He's asking you, from now until his first procedure, there's no medication for him?" Andrew said.

"Correct. No Temodar. No Avastin. The chemotherapy interferes with getting the immune system activated. We have to stop and get all the chemotherapy out so that the white blood cells are very strong when we give the vaccine. Right now he's detoxing."

"Detoxing. Okay," Mr. Tao said.

"If he wants to go back to Hong Kong, when would be a good time?" Andrew asked.

"Probably right after the last vaccine, Mr. Tao. Six weeks. You're doing good. Be strong."

"Yes!" he replied with a smile that seemed perhaps a little forced. "For our team! We are team! Strong!"

"Is it all right now if he takes fish oil?" Andrew asked.

"That's fine."

"Lycopene?"

"Fine."

"And melatonin?"

"That's fine, too."

"He's taking that in high doses," his sister added.

"Still fine," I replied.

These are all naturopathic or homeopathic treatments. If a patient comes to me and says, "Doc, I'm taking this shark cartilage because I really think it's going to help," I'll say, "Fine. Take the shark cartilage." As long as they tell me what they are taking, and as long as the substance is not harmful, it's not a problem. Lycopene is a natural antioxidant—it's what makes tomatoes red. Mr. Tao's fish oil contains omega-3 fatty acids, which have been shown to enhance immune activity. In combination with the vaccine, it could potentially help fight his tumor. It is in fact the same fish oil I'd worked with when I was still a resident at the University of Michigan in the late 1970s.

With some holistic remedies, however, timing is everything. We do have to be careful with supplements and herbal medicines, because under certain circumstances they can work against traditional treatments. Melatonin, for instance, has been shown to slow down cell division. While this effect can help stabilize tumor growth, melatonin is not something we want to give a patient who is undergoing radiation therapy, because radiation works by killing rapidly dividing cells. I had told Mr. Tao earlier to hold off on the melatonin while he was undergoing radiation treatment. Now that he was finished with radiation, it was something he could take.

There can be genuine beneficial effects from these natural remedies, but they are not necessarily as potent or as uniformly effective as they could be. Most of our pharmaceutical drugs are from plants or derivatives of plants. Coumadin, a blood thinner, comes from clover. Aspirin is made from the bark of the willow.

As valuable as those discoveries are, we don't ask patients to gnaw on a hunk of willow bark when they have a headache. Once we find something that we think works, we try to refine and intensify it to either make it more active or to target it more closely to the receptor site.

Pharmacology is really just herbal medicine, only more concentrated and more precise. If we believe that the bark of a particular type of evergreen shows promise in treating cancer, we can grind up that tree bark and give it to you, and you may get some benefit out of it. On the other hand, we could take that bark into the lab and figure out why it works. When we start, we may not know exactly what the helpful component may be, but the one thing we know going in is that not everything in that bark is therapeutic. If I can isolate that substance, concentrate it, and give it to you, the effect is going to be much more consistent, much more controlled, and probably much more effective. That's the way a cancer drug called Taxol was developed, which comes from the bark of *Taxus brevifolia*, the Pacific yew tree.

The value of naturopathy to an individual may well depend on what level we are at in the science—and where you are in the progress of your disease. As physicians and scientists, we want to isolate the compound that is proving to be of value so that we can give it to you in a very consistent way. As a patient, if your cancer is already advanced, you may not have time to wait for us to do that. And that is when many people turn to alternative or complementary medicine.

My position is that I don't view it as an either/or situation. There is a definite place in traditional Western medicine for Chinese herbal remedies like the ones Mr. Tao is taking, as well as other forms of alternative medicine. To a large extent, what people view as holistic or naturopathic or complementary medicine is really just the outskirts of conventional medicine. It's like the wild frontier that has not yet been fully explored. It is not contradictory to traditional medicine; it's just sort of the ill-defined border zones of where we are.

Although our Western research-based knowledge of treatment for brain cancers has grown rapidly in the past few years, there is still a lot we don't understand. In various holistic treatments, there are things as a scientist I can explain, and there are things as a scientist I cannot explain. The National Institutes of Health has established the National Center for Complementary and Alternative

Medicine to explore the usefulness of various alternative therapies, including Chinese and Indian (Ayurvedic) medicine, yoga, mushrooms, Qigong, reiki, massage, meditation, and other "medical and health care practices outside the realm of conventional medicine."

For many years prior to Mr. Tao's surgery, we had a very astute practitioner of complementary medicine at Cedars-Sinai, one to whom I often referred patients. His name was Evan Ross, and he was a very special individual with a practice devoted primarily to acupuncture and oriental medicine. Evan was a three-time cancer survivor himself. His first bout with cancer—a retinoblastoma, diagnosed in 1972, when Evan was two—cost him an eye. Twenty-two years later, in 1994, he was diagnosed with a brain tumor—a GBM. At that time, Evan Ross was an award-winning music producer and an avid martial artist. After two surgeries, high-dose chemotherapy, and an array of complementary medicine modalities that he researched himself, including acupuncture, various nutritional supplements, meditation, and Qigong, which combines various breathing patterns with physical postures and motions, he emerged cancer-free in 1995.

"I didn't believe I was going to die," he told a *Los Angeles Times* interviewer in July 2004. "From the beginning . . . I believed it was about learning a set of lessons. I believed it was destined to happen. And I welcomed it as a challenge." That challenge led to a dramatic change in his life.

"I spent two days in a tepee with a shaman," he later wrote. "While he by no means guaranteed my recovery, I consider my time with him to be a major turning point in my recovery. I changed from being a powerless victim of circumstance to an unusual soul who had been given the chance to transform his life in a trial by fire."

Evan left the music business, which he loved, and enrolled in the Emperor's College of Traditional Oriental Medicine in Santa Monica. He completed the course of study and became a board-certified acupuncturist and a doctor of oriental medicine, licensed in two states. He was appointed complementary medicine adviser to the National Brain Tumor Foundation, and served on the board of directors for the Center for Integrative Health, with full staff privileges at Cedars-Sinai. A longtime cancer survivor, he died in 2007 from a recurrence of his glioblastoma multiforme.

I had sent numerous patients to Dr. Ross, and one of his treatments particularly intrigued me. This was his use of maitake mushrooms (*Grifola frondosa*), which Mr. Tao would be taking with his vaccine. Dr. Ross was a big believer in maitake mushrooms, and he made me a believer as well. In recent vaccine trials, when we went back and looked at the records of patients we had referred to him, we found that those who had taken the maitake mushrooms with the vaccine did a lot better. Their survival appeared to be longer than patients who got either the maitake mushrooms alone, or the vaccine alone, which suggested to us that the combination of the two had a synergistic effect. Maitakes boost the body's immune response, and activate the macrophages, the body's scavenging white cells, which in turn devour tumor cells.

To be sure, consuming the mushrooms themselves is taking medication at a very primitive level—like chewing willow bark in lieu of taking an aspirin. The more effective we become with our treatments, the less we rely on homeopathics. When we can isolate the pure molecule that is in the mushrooms, what you really want to do is take that. And the more advanced we get in science, obviously the more we move toward that.

I sent Mr. Tao off for his blood work. After that, all we could do was wait for Gentao Liu to tell us whether or not he'd be able to make the dendritic vaccine—William Tao's own personal formulation of Anti-Tumor Juice.

Suzane Brian, my physician's assistant, kept checking with Gentao, and after two weeks he finally confirmed that the vaccine was a go. William Tao would be getting his ATJ—the new, improved synthetic version of the vaccine, which we had just brought into trials. For Suzane it was not a moment too soon. Ever since the blood was drawn, various members of the Tao extended family had been anxiously calling her at all hours, waiting to hear whether the vaccine trial could go forward.

Mr. Tao would be only the third person to be initiated into the new trial. In the previous trials, we fed the dendritic cells a vast array of tumor antigens, or peptides, which we had harvested from the patients' tumors. We expected the dendritic cells to sort through them and absorb the right peptides—the cancer-identifying proteins—though other peptides could also be absorbed. We thought there might be a better way, and eventually we were able to combine our research findings from the first vaccine study with the findings of other researchers such as Dr. Steven Rosenberg of the National Cancer Institute to develop what we hoped would be a more concentrated, more targeted vaccine. The new, improved vaccine would feed the dendritic cells only those peptides that we knew would activate the killer T-cells. It was an example of how our bench-to-bedside translational approach was being put into practice, and we hoped it would be a better cocktail for activating our patients' T-cells against their tumors.

I came in to see Mr. Tao before he got his vaccine, and I was struck by the difference that a couple of weeks had made in his morale. This time I heard laughter as I entered the room, which as usual was crowded with family members. "You look better, Mr. Tao," I said.

"Much better! I did what you say, Dr. Black," said Mr. Tao, smiling proudly. "I let her go."

I noticed one unfamiliar face. "This is my uncle, my mother's brother," Mr. Tao's sister said.

"I just come back from Las Vegas," said Mr. Tao with a grin. "I made little money, just little money."

"In his case, 'little money' is $87,000," noted the uncle

wryly. The comment brought gales of laughter from everyone in the room, Mr. Tao included.

"It's good to hear you laugh," I said. "Laughter is very healthy."

William Tao threw his arms over his head in his familiar "touchdown" sign of victory.

"Don't move, Mr. Tao!" said Suzane with a smile. "You're in the perfect position to receive the injection."

The dendritic vaccine he was about to receive in his armpit sprang from our strategy to "think like a tumor." Cancer behaves very much like a shark. It just eats and sleeps and makes more sharks. It's not going to waste any energy on something it feels is insignificant. One of the first things a cancer does to survive in the brain is to make itself invisible to the immune system, to hide its cancer scent so our immune system cannot recognize it as a cancer cell and kill it before it is able to divide and grow. In addition to hiding from our immune system, cancer cells release chemicals around them to kill off attacking immune cells. Cancer spends so much energy trying to evade the immune system that it occurred to us that it wouldn't do that without a reason. The reason, we believe, is that the tumor knows that if the immune system can be activated against it, the cancer could be eradicated.

More support for our theory that an immune attack could kill brain cancer cells came from another "odd observation." We had noticed that statistically, the strongest predictor of survival in brain cancer patients is age, or rather, the lack of it. A twenty-year-old with a malignant Grade 4 glioblastoma has pretty much the same prognosis as an eighty-year-old patient with a low Grade 2 tumor. In addition to his holistic therapies, his youth may have been a key reason why Evan Ross had been a long-term survivor of GBM.

We had known about the age factor for decades; we just didn't know why it happened. I asked Chris Wheeler, our immunologist, to take that bedside observation back to the lab bench and figure out why age mattered so much. He found that younger patients have more T-cells that can be deployed against the tumor. These discoveries have led to our development of the dendritic cell vaccine—which gets more T-cells activated and recruited into the fight against brain cancer.

We zeroed in on the development of a treatment that would strengthen the immune system. Even when we had the concept, the most challenging thing was to bring it out of the lab and into clinical trials—to go from rats to human beings. It took a lot of time and a multidisciplinary effort to get to the point where we could offer the dendritic vaccine in clinical trials to patients like Glenn Rhoades and William Tao. We also needed to have clinical manufacturing capability. All of this costs money, but government funding and/or pharmaceutical company investment in this kind of research does not take place until development of a treatment is pretty far down the road.

Government money, specifically a research grant from the National Institutes of Health, is usually not forthcoming until "proof of concept" has been demonstrated. "Proof of concept" means that we can demonstrate feasibility; in other words, we can show that it will work. Like other federal institutions, the NIH has a narrow profile in terms of what grants they award, because they are "giving away" taxpayer dollars. As much as anyone may deplore wasteful government spending, what this means for us in the research lab is that long before we get to "proof of concept," we have to find other ways to fund our work in the early going.

One might think that pharmaceutical companies would fund the development of new treatments, but they do not, at least not in the preliminary stages. Large drug manufacturers used to do their own research. Today, they've become more like marketing firms. Before they will get involved, we have to show them the same kind of feasibility we show the NIH. We have to remove their risk by doing the necessary animal and early Phase I and Phase II human trials ourselves. These demonstrate safety and effectiveness, which is where we are at with the dendritic vaccine today. Only after we can show that our clinical trials have been successful will they plunk down the $300 to $400 million that is needed to take the idea through the final Phase III trials to FDA approval.

That hefty price tag to get across the finish line puts a very cold spin on how the merit of medical breakthroughs is assessed. Not only does the treatment have to work for patients on a case-by-case basis, it also has to work at the corporate bottom line. The high cost of bringing a cancer treatment to market tends to push its evaluation out of *risk-benefit* mode and into *cost-benefit* mode.

That may sound hard, but it's realistic—if you are the CEO of the pharmaceutical company paying those huge Phase III bills, you want some reasonable assurance that you'll be able to recoup that $300 to $400 million over time. Your responsibility is to your stockholders. With a brain tumor vaccine, you may never get it. There are approximately 22,000 new cases of primary malignant brain tumors each year. As a neurosurgeon, I think that's too many. But if I'm that CEO of the drug company, I think maybe it's not enough. Without a sufficient number of tumor patients, I may never sell enough vaccine to earn back our development cost, let alone make money.

A pharmaceutical company wants an off-the-shelf product that it can easily package and sell to patients with brain malignancies—for them, the definition of "proof of concept" includes an element of economic viability. Our dendritic vaccine is not there yet; it still has to be custom-manufactured for each patient. The new synthetic vaccine trial that William Tao is participating in is an important step toward developing a product that could eventually be marketed this way, but we still have a way to go.

It has cost us somewhere between $15 to $20 million

to get the dendritic vaccine this far, but that does not completely account for the money we spent on other ideas before we concluded that they wouldn't pan out. For every ten concepts that researchers pursue in the lab, only one will ultimately prove to be worthwhile. Sometimes we get lucky and find low-hanging fruit—drugs that are already FDA approved. This was what happened with Levitra, which had already been approved for erectile dysfunction at the time we started testing it on the blood-brain barrier. In most cases, though, we are starting from ground zero. We have to be proficient at cherry-picking the prospective winners early on; the less spent on false starts the better. This is why we so avidly hunt for the odd observations—they are the ones most likely to pay off.

How can we afford to do this? Only with tremendous donor and hospital support. Although we have received many research grants from the National Institutes of Health, NIH funding may be increasingly hard to come by in the future. For the past several years, the NIH budget has been essentially flat in terms of dollars, which means that it has been declining relative to inflation. There is also more competition than ever for those dwindling resources. It may take me three months to write a solid NIH proposal, but the probability of getting funded is no better than 7 or 8 percent.

Those are not good odds, so we must rely on other sources for the monies we need for the early phases of our research. More than half of our funding comes from an active fund-raising program, and from Cedars-Sinai itself. As it has from the beginning in 1997, the hospital returns a portion of the fees we generate for use in our research efforts.

Our Brain Trust raises money both for the Maxine Dunitz Neurosurgical Institute, and for our new Johnnie L. Cochran, Jr., Brain Tumor Center. Established in 2007, the Cochran Center is named after my dear friend who died of a glioblastoma multiforme in 2005. Launched with more than $5 million in donations, including a generous contribution from the Cochran family, the Center serves as the nerve center and coordination hub for everyone involved in clinical trials, from physicians to data managers to research nurses. It will help us fast-track the route from bench to bedside for promising new treatments.

What causes brain cancer? What determines who it strikes? It appears to be a balance between environmental and genetic factors. Glenn Rhoades was able to document his exposure to any number of toxic substances during his childhood and teen years, including the very air he breathed. That said, not everyone who grew up in smoggy Riverside, California, in the 1960s has developed an anaplastic astrocytoma. Cell phones have been implicated in the type of tumor that Johnnie Cochran had, a GBM. From the earliest days when cell phones were first available to the public, Johnnie was a heavy cell phone user. Studies have shown a correlation between the side that a patient uses their cell phone and the side of the brain where their glioblastoma occurs, a correlation I've noticed in a great many of my patients. Other studies have shown a higher risk of developing GBMs with heavy cell phone use as well as the development of a benign tumor that develops close to the hearing, or eighth, nerve, the type of tumor discovered in the young woman you will meet in the next chapter. To date there has been insufficient rigorous scientific exploration concerning this phenomenon, but it is surely an odd observation worth pursuing.

CHAPTER 10

Cellular Signs

Everyone just wants to gamma knife me!" my new patient complained as I introduced myself to her. Clad in upscale jogging attire and peeking out from behind a pair of oversize designer sunglasses, the attractive young woman was accompanied by her mother. "Either that or cut my hearing!" she continued.

She had been diagnosed with a vestibular schwannoma, sometimes called an acoustic neuroma, and she was here to discuss the risks and benefits of various treatment options. The name "vestibular schwannoma" is indeed a mouthful, but it is derived from the location where the tumor most often begins. This is a nonmalignant tumor of the eighth cranial nerve, also known as the vestibulocochlear nerve, which governs hearing and balance, and often originates in the cells that sheathe the nerve, which are called Schwann cells. Eventually these tumors can become large enough to push on the brain stem and on other cranial nerves. They usually grow quite slowly, but because of their location, vestibular schwannomas can be difficult to remove surgically.

My patient already understood how hard it was going to be; she'd previously consulted with a number of other doctors. "Where my tumor is isn't pretty," she declared, "especially given what I do for a living. And everything they want to do to fix it is gonna give me a problem. Let me see . . . to get rid of the tumor, you're going to take away my balance, take away my hearing, *and* take away my face?? I don't think so."

My patient's name is Tionne Watkins, and she is in the entertainment business. Sometimes called T-Boz, she first became known as one-third of the extremely successful R&B/hip-hop trio TLC. To date, the group has sold over 45 million recordings worldwide, and remains among the best-selling female singing groups of all time. Twice named to *People* magazine's annual list of most beautiful people, at this point in her life, Tionne was hoping to branch out into an on-camera television career. For her, any treatment option that carried a significant risk of loss of balance, loss of hearing, or loss of facial mobility would take away her livelihood.

This was the same tumor that another patient of mine, Elishadie Tezera, had had, but Tionne had one additional issue that made treating her tumor far more challenging. Tionne suffers from sickle-cell disease. About 70,000 people in the United States have it; most of them are African-Americans.

Millions more have sickle-cell trait, meaning they carry the recessive sickle-cell gene. Although people with the trait generally have no symptoms, they may pass the gene on to their offspring. Children who receive the gene from both parents will be afflicted with the disease itself.

Sickle-cell disease (also called sickle-cell anemia) is a congenital blood disorder characterized by malformation of the red blood cells. Rather than looking like lifesavers—discs with a slightly flattened center—the cells are bent and elongated, like tiny boomerangs. Unlike healthy red blood cells, they are inflexible, and their inflexibility makes them unable to squeeze through the body's smallest blood vessels, the capillaries. When sickle cells dam up in the capillaries, they create logjams that cut off the flow of blood and oxygen to tissues and organs downstream. These sickle-cell attacks are potentially life-threatening, intensely painful, and can result in permanent organ damage. There is as yet no cure. Tionne had been in and out of hospitals all her life. Now in her mid-thirties, at one point she was not expected to see her thirtieth birthday.

"Sickle-cell isn't the easiest thing, but I've dealt with it," she said. "I used to go into the hospital every three months. The last bad episode I had, I was hospitalized for four months straight. I'm one of those people who they said would be on disability, but I overcame everything. I've traveled the world, singing and dancing and working hard," she declared. "When they told me about the tumor, I wasn't going to let that stop me, either."

"Can you tell me how it was discovered?" I asked.

"I'd started having these headaches. At first I didn't think much of it—I've had them for years. I'd take some meds, or get massages to de-stress myself, but over the past few months it started getting to the point where nothing was working. My mother and my boyfriend, Takeo Spikes, kept bugging me to go get an MRI. Takeo is an NFL linebacker, and he'd just lost a family member to brain cancer, so he was highly sensitized to what the downside might be. He said, 'You have *waaay* too many headaches, and there's too much technology out there. Go.' "

"Your boyfriend gave you good advice," I said.

"My mother was on my case, too," she continued. "They both were—and they were relentless. Finally it got to the point where the pain in my butt was as bad as the pain in my head, so I went." Tionne's comment brought a smile and a nod from her mom.

"And then you went for an MRI scan?" I asked.

"Yes, but a few days later, I still hadn't heard anything, so I called my hematologist. Because of the sickle-cell, he's sort of my go-to everything doc. He called me back on my cell and said, 'T, where you at?'

" 'I'm out shopping,' I told him.

" 'You need to go home and call me back,' he replied.

"I told him, 'No. I don't want to go home and call you back. I'm not going to get into a wreck on the highway. Just tell me—I have a brain tumor, right?'

" 'Right,' he said, 'but I don't think it's cancerous.'

"He called it by its long scientific name, vestibular schwannoma," Tionne said. "Then he got real technical, telling me the location, the size—1.8 centimeters—and all that. I was pulling scraps of paper out of my purse and scribbling as fast as I could, so I could tell whoever I went to see exactly what I've got, so I could be thorough. Then tears came to my eyes. I was so worried that it was going to be malignant. I started thinking, 'I've got this thing that I can't even spell or pronounce, and it could kill me.' Chase, my daughter, is only six years old. I have to be here for her."

"The vestibular schwannoma is not malignant," I explained, "but that's not the same as saying it's benign. Although your tumor will not spread to other areas of the brain, as it continues to grow, it will have ever-increasing adverse effects. The first symptoms people generally notice include hearing impairment, usually on one side only, facial numbness, unsteadiness or imbalance, vertigo, or, as in your case, persistent headache." Tionne needed treatment of the tumor or it could eventually prove to be fatal.

"I went to a specialist in Atlanta," she said, making a face of disapproval. "I totally didn't like him. I have a thing about doctors—they have to have a certain connection with me, and they have to care about me—as a person. I don't want them treating me like a symptom, or a disease; I need them to care about me, about my feelings, and to care about what I'm going through. Nobody explained anything to me—they didn't even show me the

MRIs. They just wanted to gamma knife my head. Well, that and take my check. That's how I felt."

It should not be surprising that patients with brain tumors may have a heightened intolerance for impersonal medical care. Tionne, perhaps because she'd already spent so much of her life dealing with doctors and hospitals, knew what good care was, and was not satisfied with anything less. She also knew how to find what she needed.

"As a patient, you have to do the research yourself," she said. "I went on the Internet; I made phone calls. Takeo helped. I looked up the gamma knife; I looked up the surgery, and found all these different approaches. The more I researched, the more difference of opinion I found."

While looking into treatment options for her tumor, Tionne had discovered what many of my patients find: The Internet, while full of information, can also be full of contradiction. For vestibular schwannomas, the conflicting advice to patients on the Web mirrors what has been an active and at times heated discussion in the professional literature among neurosurgeons, radiation oncologists, and otolaryngologists about the best way to treat this particular tumor.

Some sites on the Internet suggest using the gamma knife to treat almost every tumor; others advocate surgery, going through the ear in what is known as the translabyrinthine approach. Some believe that this technique offers better odds for saving the facial nerve, but it carries an unavoidable downside. In the translabyrinthine approach, surgeons must drill out the middle ear, which inevitably results in complete hearing loss on the operative side of the head. For a number of patients, however, this is not as much of a negative as it may appear. By the time they are diagnosed with a vestibular schwannoma, a significant number of people have already lost some or all of their hearing. In many of these cases, there has already been irreversible nerve damage—and hence permanent hearing loss—that removal of the tumor cannot undo. For these individuals, sacrificing hearing to save the facial nerve is a less onerous choice.

A third surgical technique is known as the retrosigmoid or suboccipital approach. It is a more challenging surgery, but offers the best chance to preserve both hearing and facial mobility. This was the surgery Tionne was hoping we could offer her.

At Cedars-Sinai we evaluate every person individually. Working as an interdisciplinary team, we then determine what we believe to be the best approach for that patient. We each bring our own particular expertise to this analysis. Like a mini–Tumor Board, the team includes advocates of each approach. I work with our gamma knife specialist, and often with neuro-otologist Dr. Rick Friedman of the House Ear Institute in Los Angeles. Dr. Friedman is an ear, nose, and throat surgeon specializing in the treatment of vestibular schwannomas. He is part of the team that developed the translabyrinthine approach.

I sat with Tionne and her mother, going over the pros

and cons of the various ways we could treat her tumor, and answering all of their questions as forthrightly as I could. "The advantage of the gamma knife," I explained, "is that it does not require surgery. It is performed on an outpatient basis, and has a 90 percent chance of preventing the tumor from getting larger. It does, however, carry a risk of causing facial weakness, hearing loss, or brainstem damage from radiation injury, which usually occur about a year after the treatment."

Tionne shook her head vigorously. She wanted no part of the gamma knife. "I saw that the tumor can come back malignant," she said. "Years after, you can end up messed up anyway. Your balance, hearing, and facial nerves might still go out in five, ten, twenty years. And you can burn the brain stem." From her research, Tionne also knew that if the gamma knife treatment failed and the tumor continued to grow, the risk of injury to the facial and other nerves, as well as to the brain stem, would be much higher due to scarring from the radiation treatment. That scarring might also render future surgeries much more difficult.

She also wanted nothing to do with the translabyrinthine approach. Tionne fortunately still had her hearing, and she was also still a recording artist. She needed her hearing on both sides. For her, the translabyrinthine approach was out.

From a career standpoint, Tionne's tumor showed up at a most inopportune time. "I'd just been offered the deal of a lifetime," she explained. "ABC and Buena Vista were going to put me on daytime television. It was going to be me and Chilli [Rozonda Thomas, the other surviving member of TLC]," she continued. "The check from ABC was on the table. I was supposed to shoot the pilot for the show. Right when the contract was done, I found out I had the tumor.

"I don't want to sing forever. I haven't really cared about the music world in years. I was sitting home happy, taking my daughter to school, fixing school lunches, doing normal people things. I was into it, because I never got the chance to do that when we were singing. I'm thirty-six; I've been singing since I was nineteen. I just wanted to be normal for a second.

"I got real stressed thinking about it, because I thought I might never see another check like this again in my life—and I have a daughter to support. It was going to be a great opportunity for me. It would open a lot of doors and take my career in a new direction. The whole thing was driving me crazy. The stress of it could have sent me into a sickle-cell crisis. My stomach was hurting . . ."

"Tionne, I think your body was talking to you," said her mom.

"Exactly. Knowing my situation, I couldn't sign the contract and take the money. I didn't want to go into a deal knowing that I'd told a lie, or that I was hiding something. A lot of people in my business would have signed the contract and then said, 'Oh, by the way, I have a brain tumor.' I couldn't do that. For me, it would have been deceitful, and on top of it, I didn't feel good in my heart. I didn't think it was something God would have wanted me to do."

"What did you do?" I asked.

"I had to get it off my chest. I called the executives at ABC/Buena Vista and told them what was going on. They couldn't have been better about it. Very supportive. They put off the show for a year. I don't know what's going to happen, but I have a contract waiting for me as soon as I get better."

After seeing numerous other specialists, Tionne found us at Cedars-Sinai. She wanted surgery that would spare both her hearing and her facial nerve, but because of her sickle-cell disease, no one she had consulted thus far had been willing to attempt it. I looked at her situation differently. In many ways, I actually saw Tionne as an ideal candidate for surgery. She was young, and although the tumor was compressing the auditory nerve, she still had her hearing.

Unquestionably, the operation was going to be a ten out of ten on the degree-of-difficulty scale. Going in to save both hearing and the facial nerve is about as tough as it gets. I reviewed the risks of the operation with her, including the possible risk of hearing loss, facial paralysis, and the other risks associated with brain surgery. Although her tumor was compressing the auditory nerve, I was confident I could achieve an image-complete resection and bring her out of the OR with all of her cranial nerves intact. The problem would be to get her through the inevitable post-op sickle-cell crisis.

Tionne did not hesitate. After conferring briefly with her mother, she told me she wanted to go forward with the operation, even if it triggered a sickle-cell attack. "I know I'm a walking miracle," she declared. "I've been through enough already to be able to deal with it. I'm not coming here trying to be the superstar person. I was told I couldn't have kids, and now I feel I've got to be here for my baby. I'm just Tionne the mother who wants to make it back alive and in one piece."

If you go by the literature, the odds of saving Tionne's hearing were not in our favor. Most neurosurgical papers report that useful hearing can only be saved in 10 to 20 percent of patients with tumors the size of Tionne's, and the risk of hearing loss is directly related to the size of the tumor. We had to do much better than those odds, and I was confident that we would. I had saved hearing with tumors much larger. One patient with a very large vestibular schwannoma actually had improved hearing after her tumor was removed.

The main problem was going to be the threat of a sickle-cell crisis. To give Tionne the best possible chance of fighting it off, we transfused and hydrated her blood prior to surgery. This gave her a lot more fluid volume in the blood, and diluted her abnormal sickle cells with normal disc-shaped red cells, making the capillary logjam less likely, and decreasing its severity should it occur.

Assisting me the morning of Tionne's surgery were Geno Hunt and Dr. Rick Friedman. Dr. Friedman would be doing the drilling to widen the internal auditory canal. We were taking every precaution to protect Tionne's hearing and her facial functions. After she was under anesthesia, we placed speakers in both ears that would produce clicking sounds throughout the surgery. These clicking sounds would be transmitted to her inner ear, where they would be converted to electrical waves that would travel up the hearing pathways in her brain stem to her brain. Electrodes were then placed over her scalp to detect these electrical impulses. The impulses travel rapidly to the brain in a characteristic five-wave pattern and at a predictable speed. In the OR, these brain-stem auditory evoked responses, or BAERS (pronounced "bears"), as they are called, would be constantly monitored by a specially trained technician. During surgery, any slowing of these waves, or any decrease in their size would immediately tell us that the hearing nerve or the brain stem was in danger.

To protect Tionne's facial nerve, small electrode needles were placed at numerous points in her face to aid in locating the facial nerve within her brain. As I operated, I would stimulate various areas within the tumor. If her facial muscles twitched, that would tell me that the facial nerve was in the vicinity.

My job would be to locate the tiny thread-like facial and hearing nerves within the tumor, and to remove the tumor without damaging them. I also had to stay clear of her brain stem. In other words, I was back in Tiger Country, and this was a job that needed all my skills as a thief in the night.

Tionne's positioning on the operating table was critical. To get to her tumor, we would need access to the area between her cerebellum and her skull on the right side of her head. We set her up so she was lying on her left side, which meant that the tumor side of her head was facing upward.

It was 7:00 a.m. when we began. The incision we used for entry into Tionne's brain was hidden behind her hairline and less than an inch long. It would be virtually undetectable. Combing her hair over the area would easily conceal the small, narrow band of hair we shaved around the incision. No one would know from looking at her that she'd had brain surgery, even right after she went home.

To enter the skull, we used a high-speed drill to create a small opening, about the size of a dime. The dura mater was then separated from the skull, and a bone drill was used to cut out a wider window of bone just above a very large vein called the sigmoid sinus. It all had to be highly precise or Tionne could have been in danger of bleeding to death. It was also possible that air might have been sucked into the vein and gone to the lungs, which could have resulted in cardiac arrest.

There was no room for error. I made the incision in the dura just one millimeter away from the vein. I had to get as close as possible in order to get the best angle of approach to the tumor. I then cut a small opening in the arachnoid mater, the clear, thin membrane covering the brain, to release the cerebrospinal fluid. As the crystal-clear liquid drained, the cerebellum became very relaxed and began to fall away from the skull. This is where gravity became our friend and ally, and why positioning on the table had been so important. When we opened the arachnoid mater and drained the CSF, the force of gravity pulled Tionne's cerebellum downward, giving us a nice corridor to get to the tumor and get it out. In a sense, we were able to retract her cerebellum without having to touch or manipulate it. Physical retraction would have brought with it a risk of brain damage.

Focusing the microscope deeper into the space between the skull and the cerebellum, I could now clearly see the tumor. Part of it was growing into the canal where the seventh and eighth cranial nerves exit the skull, heading for her inner ear. My strategy in attacking these tumors is to get the tumor out of the canal first, and then find the other end of the facial and hearing nerves as they leave the brain stem. Dr. Friedman began his part of the surgery, drilling to widen the internal auditory canal.

"I'm getting a small delay on the BAERS," the technician announced over the quiet of the operating room. Rick stopped drilling. "Okay," the technician reported after a moment, "BAERS back to baseline." Dr. Friedman resumed drilling out the canal.

"Let's have stimulation," Rick said, calling for the facial nerve stimulator. "Point one millivolts."

Tick, tick, tick, tick . . .

"Okay, getting facial stimulation," he said. One hour after he began drilling, he located the facial nerve exiting the far end of the inner ear.

Rick stepped back from the microscope. "Okay," he said, "we're ready for you." That was my signal to take over. "I got into a few air cells," he added as I moved in to take my place at the microscope.

"Okay," I said.

There are air cells in the bones around the canal that connect to the middle ear. If these air cells are opened, they can allow cerebrospinal fluid to leak out of the brain and into the nose. The leak is a potential danger, because cerebrospinal fluid is rich in sugar, which bacteria in the nose love. The problem is that the CSF could serve as a conduit for nasal bacteria to find their way back into the brain, causing a life-threatening infection.

Looking through the microscope, I found the air cells Rick had drilled into. "Bone wax," I requested. Bone wax is a sterile mixture of beeswax and a softening agent such as petroleum jelly or paraffin. It can be easily molded to a desired shape without heating. The scrub nurse handed me a small dab of bone wax on a long micro dissector, and I carefully plugged the air cells with it.

I now repositioned the microscope, focusing directly on the tumor, then zoomed in for higher magnification. The objective: to find the facial and hearing nerves as they exited Tionne's brain stem. To do that without touching the cerebellum or the brain stem, I would first need to gut out the inner mass of the tumor, leaving its exterior shell or capsule intact. Without the inner mass to sustain its shape, the tumor would then collapse or involute, caving in on itself.

I knew that somewhere in the very thin fraction-of-a-millimeter capsule of the tumor was the facial nerve. Even though I could not see it, I knew it was there. The facial nerve, which is normally very small and thin to begin with, now gets splayed out like wet tissue paper over the tumor, very thin, and very, very fragile. I needed to enter the tumor capsule and empty it out without cutting the nerve, so I focused the microscope on an area where it was least likely for it to be hiding.

"How are the BAERS?" I asked.

"All five waves are good. No change from baseline," the technician replied.

"Facial nerve stimulator at point two millivolts," I requested.

"Point two millivolts," the technician replied.

I moved the long needle-like stimulator over an area of the tumor capsule that I had tentatively picked as my entry point.

"Stimulate."

Click, click, click, click . . .

"No facial nerve. Good. Stimulation off. Suction. Irrigation please."

The stimulation had confirmed that the facial nerve was not in the area of the tumor capsule I had selected.

The scrub tech handed me the micro scissors, and I cut into the fleshy capsule of the tumor. Using the Decker forceps and taking great care not to damage the overlaying capsule, I carefully began to gut the tumor from the inside out.

"No delay in the BAERS," the technician reported. The hearing nerve was still intact. As the tumor began to shrink, I could now see the fifth (trigeminal) cranial nerve passing over the top of the tumor. I carefully separated it from the capsule. Several small but critical arteries supplying blood to the brain stem were also stretched over the tumor capsule. Under the microscope they looked like very fine mesh netting, but any damage to them could cause a devastating brain-stem stroke. Some of the arteries were not simply sitting on top of the capsule; instead, they were stuck to it. I very carefully developed a thin dissection plane between the arachnoid tissue layers separating the brain from the tumor, layers so thin I could barely discern them under the microscope. Using a Rhoton 3 micro dissector, which looks like a microscopic pancake spatula on a very long handle, I carefully manipulated the arteries away from the tumor.

"Stimulation at point two millivolts."

Click, click, click . . .

"No facial."

The brain stem was now coming into view. I could see the ninth (glossopharyngeal), tenth (vagus), and eleventh (accessory) cranial nerves that govern our ability to taste, to swallow, to feel heat and pain, to regulate our heartbeat, and other critical functions. The nerves were just below the tumor, which had attached itself to the brain stem. This was the darkest heart of Tiger Country. Again, I very carefully developed the thin arachnoid plane between the brain stem and the tumor capsule. Under the microscope I could see the delicate latticework of blood vessels covering the brain stem, all of which absolutely had to be preserved. The technician watching the TV monitor could see I was now working along the brain stem.

"No change in BAERS," he said, reassuring me that the brain stem was unharmed. The whole team was in the zone now. The scrub tech passed me the instruments I needed, most of the time without my saying a word. This is surgery at its best—when the entire surgical team is focused and working as one.

As I worked to develop a plane between the tumor capsule and the brain stem, I knew I had to be getting close to the facial nerve.

"Stimulator at point one millivolts," I said.

As I moved the stimulator needle along the brain stem and the tumor capsule, I could hear the familiar *click*, *click*, *click*. Then came a different pitch: *tick*, *tick*, *tick*.

"Positive for facial nerve stimulation," the technician reported.

I still couldn't see the facial nerve, but the stimulator told me it was there: hiding, almost invisible between the tumor capsule and the brain stem. As I dialed up the magnification on the surgical microscope, I could just make out the faint outline of the seventh cranial nerve—the facial nerve—and beyond it, barely visible, the fibers of the eighth cranial nerve—the vestibulocochlear nerve. I would spend the next hour carefully separating these two nerves away from the tumor, following them all the way into the canal that Rick had widened earlier.

Finally the tumor was out. I stimulated the facial nerve one more time at the brain stem to make sure that it was intact and working.

Tick, tick, tick . . .

"Strong facial response," the technician reported.

"Good," I replied. I irrigated the brain with saline. The saline flowed clear out of the surgical opening—there was no sign of bleeding. We took one last look at the incredible anatomy around the human brain stem. It really was God's artwork.

It was one o'clock in the afternoon. Tionne's operation had taken six hours, but it looked like there was good news all around. Serguei had reported the tumor we sent him was consistent with a benign schwannoma; all cranial nerves were intact; the brain stem was preserved; no blood vessels were damaged. The BAERS had remained unchanged during the entire course of the surgery, and that was a very good sign indeed.

Twenty-six years ago, as a young intern, I had watched a surgical team take thirty-two hours to remove a vestibular schwannoma. The patient survived the operation, but was neurologically devastated. I thought briefly on how far we'd come in just a generation. We wouldn't know for certain till we saw Tionne in Recovery, but there was every indication that she was going to be fine.

Now it was time to close. After we got a good watertight seal on her dura, small titanium plates were used to anchor the portion of Tionne's skull we had removed back in place. The scalp was then closed in layers with a subcutaneous plastic surgery closure that would not leave a scar. No one would know that we had ever been there.

The thief in the night had made a clean getaway. As I left the operating room, I said thank you to everyone for a job well done.

When Tionne woke up in Recovery, her facial muscles were working perfectly and she could hear. She had come through the surgery with no deficits. She was doing so well we bypassed the ICU and admitted her directly from Recovery to a regular room. The next day she was walking the halls.

Now we went on high alert. Everyone involved with her care was vigilant for any signs of a sickle-cell crisis. Four days after surgery, she started having a lot of joint and knee pain. That was the beginning of her sickle-cells acting up. Thanks in part to the transfusion beforehand, however, it was not a full-blown attack, and Tionne recovered quickly.

Several weeks later she was back in my examining room for her first post-op checkup, wearing her trademark running attire and sunglasses.

"How is your hearing?" I asked her.

"Great," she said, beaming. "I'm so happy."

"And the dizziness?"

"I'm still spinning, if I move quickly. But I can deal with that."

"Vestibular schwannomas start in the balance nerve," I said. "It's not uncommon for patients to be dizzy anywhere from a day to several weeks after surgery as the inner ear readjusts."

"It's going to get better, right?" she asked.

"Absolutely. You're doing excellent," I assured her. "You can go home to Atlanta whenever you want to."

"Like tomorrow?"

"Absolutely."

"That's the best news of all!" she exclaimed, overwhelming me with a hug. "Dr. Black, do you know what caused my tumor?" she asked intently.

"We cannot say for certain," I told her, "but some data shows that it might be related to cell phone use. There is nothing conclusive as yet, but to be safe, I'm recommending that you use an earpiece to keep the cell away from the brain."

There is a great deal of discussion and indeed controversy about whether cell phones are a contributing cause of brain cancer. Cell phone manufacturers are clearly aware that there may be a potential risk. Because microwave radiation diminishes with distance, cell phone owner manuals advise us to hold the phone a certain distance from our heads. Unfortunately, not many people follow these instructions.

Cell phones are a source of microwave radiation. A large Swedish study found that individuals using cell phones for an hour a day increased their risk of brain tumors by two and a half times. In other studies in Sweden, ten years of cell phone usage doubled the risk for vestibular schwannomas, which originate in the ear canal and grow back into the brain. Another recent study by researchers in Finland found a 40 percent increase in risk for developing glioblastomas with cell phone use.

At this point, the jury is still out. In addition to these Scandinavian studies that point definitively to a relationship, there are other studies that have concluded that no relationship exists. One of the difficulties is that some tumors—vestibular schwannomas among them—typically grow rather slowly. As a result, we may need more time to prove conclusively whether there is a link between cell phone utilization and brain tumors.

There has been a huge increase in cell phone usage over the past decade, both in terms of the number of users and in terms of the amount of time the average user spends on the phone. There is every expectation that this trend will continue. A whole generation of young people uses cell phones exclusively—many in their twenties and early thirties have no landlines in their homes at all. Although research conclusions to date have been far from unanimous, we surely do not want to find out belatedly ten years from now—and millions of hours of cell phone usage later—that there is a correlation.

We certainly have enough evidence today to suggest that the prudent individual should take precautions. I am particularly concerned about the amount of time children today spend with cell phones glued to their ears. We know that because children's brains are still developing, they can be more susceptible than grown-ups to tumor formation. In the lab, it is significantly easier to induce a tumor in young rats than in adults.

I believe it is wise for parents to curtail cell phone usage in their children. Even adults, however, would be well advised to take one relatively simple step to decrease their exposure. Among my patients, I have noticed a correlation between the side of the head where the tumor appears, and the side of the head where the cell phone is generally held. The problem comes from holding the cell phone in contact with the ear, bringing the microwave radiation emitted by the device close to the brain. I use an earpiece, and I encourage my patients to do the same. As for Bluetooth devices, they are a source of some radiation themselves, and may not be as safe as a wire earpiece.

I'm often asked whether brain tumors are becoming more frequent. Unfortunately the answer is yes, even when one takes our improving ability to diagnose them into account. Tragically, many of the new victims are children: Brain cancer is now the leading cause of cancer death in people under the age of nineteen. In the next—and final—chapter, we'll explore the many potential causes of brain tumors, why their incidence is on the rise, and the new weapons we are developing to fight this terrible enemy.

CHAPTER 11

Continuing the Fight

Suzane Brian entered my office moments after I arrived to work. She looked somber, and I could tell she had been crying.

"I am so sad to have to tell you this, but Gerard Kelly has died."

I couldn't move or speak. My only thought was of how brave Gerard had been, and how supportive his brother Thomas was. They had fought the good fight.

Gerard had gotten his six months, but very little more. I knew he spent those six months surrounded by his loved ones, which in and of itself was something he found worthwhile.

It was that last bit of his tumor that we had been unable to remove. Had it regrown away from the brain stem, it might have been several years before it became life-threatening once more. Instead, it grew back into the brain stem, compressing the delicate nerve pathways that governed all of his body functions. At that point, there was nothing more that could be done. Gerard Kelly's passing was heartrending news for all of us who came to admire his courage in the face of very tough odds. His bravery was an inspiration to us all.

Gerard developed pneumonia, and then began to lose feeling. "He knew he was dying," his brother Thomas explained by phone, "but he was more worried about the rest of us and how we were going to cope than he was about himself. An hour before he died, he checked with each of us as we stood by his bedside, asking if we were okay. And then he was gone."

Was Gerard Kelly's surgery worth it? Absolutely. First there was the tumor itself, which was benign. Had there been a good surgical plane between that last piece of tumor and the brain stem, we might have been looking at a cure. Second, even knowing the rigors of the surgery and recuperation, it was what Gerard wanted. It was very clear that this young man and his family, even if the chances were very small, wanted at least the opportunity to survive.

I believe that this is the kind of case where a neurosurgeon should not play God, and playing God for me in this instance would have entailed making the choice myself and refusing to do the surgery. I was very forthright with both Gerard and his brother that the odds of significantly extending his life were maybe 5 to 10 percent. Unquestionably, it was a lot of surgery for him to go through to try for that 5- to 10-percent shot. Nevertheless, he wasn't ready to give up, and I was confident I could buy him at least another six months with the surgery.

Would I do it again? Yes. If the next Gerard Kelly came in to see me, I'd do the same thing. In countless ways both large and small, all of my patients find ways to fight their illness with the same kind of courage and determination as Gerard Kelly. My patients teach us all to stop and smell the roses, and to truly focus on what is important. They have meaningful conversations with their loved ones, and do the important things in life that those of us not facing death often never get around to. I have learned many lessons from my patients, but one lesson I will always treasure is how one can live an entire lifetime in a few years, or even a few months, and to zero in on what really matters.

And what of Scott Erdman? Scott continues to serve God and his congregation at the Hollywood Presbyterian Church. He returns annually for an MRI scan, and every year his wife, Pam, waits anxiously for the word that he is still cancer-free. For the past decade and a half, there has been nothing but good news. Scott is a demonstration of the reason why I continue to fight for patients like Gerard Kelly. At the outset, Scott, like Gerard, had been given six months to live. If I'd given up on Scott Erdman, he wouldn't be here. Who is to say whether the next Gerard Kelly will be the next Scott Erdman? And that is exactly the point: Even when we know the odds, we don't know who will be a long-term survivor and who will not.

Milagros Reid was given a course of chemotherapy with

Temodar and is responding well. She is looking forward to spending time with her grandchildren, and to getting back to work. I was not surprised that she wanted to continue working; I've come to understand how important work is to my patients. This is true across economic levels, from laborers to CEOs—even the terminally ill have a strong desire to continue contributing to society. With the chemotherapy working on her tumor, she can look forward to many years of productivity, and many years of making memories for her grandchildren.

Elishadie Tezera graduated from the University of Texas, El Paso, with a bachelor of science degree. She is now enrolled in the College of Dentistry at Howard University in Washington, D.C. It is a demanding program, with classes from eight to five every day and a lot of studying at night, but she is meeting the challenge and looking forward to becoming a dentist. "I used to be very stressed out," she said when I last spoke with her. "Now I take it all in stride."

The irrepressible Glenn Rhoades continues to enjoy his life. After completing his series of dendritic vaccine injections, he resumed chemotherapy with Temodar. Both seem to be doing their job. His MRI scans have been clear for more than a year now, and Glenn and Carol are back on the motorcycle, exploring the California coast. When I asked him how he was doing he responded, "I am generally excellent." Indeed. He recently climbed into a Cessna 182 with a friend and flew from Oceanside, about halfway between Los Angeles and San Diego, to the mountain community of

Big Bear. Big Bear is located in the San Bernardino Mountains just north of Riverside, where he grew up, and for Glenn this was a homecoming of sorts—his family had a cabin there. The two friends had breakfast in Big Bear, and then flew to Catalina Island, just off the coast, for lunch. "We had buffalo burgers there," he said, "then flew back to Oceanside."

Glenn Rhoades says that he can see himself clearly, before and after his brain tumor. Although he might stop short of calling it a "rebirth," he relishes the difference his diagnosis has made in the way he chooses to live his life. Possessions have taken a backseat to experiences. "Before, all I did was work," he confesses. "There was a time when I actually sold my vacation time for cash, just so I'd have more money to invest or buy some stuff. It was just stuff, stuff, and more stuff. I still love my stuff, but I have a completely different attitude toward all of the young folk in my family—nieces, nephews, my children. I take a lot of time to help them now. I'll do what I can to assist them through all of their challenges. For me, having fun and focusing on things that are just plain more enjoyable has been a big change."

William Tao is still fighting, but his brave battle against his deadly adversary sadly seems to be nearing its end. The stress from his impending divorce and legal action against him may well have contributed to a regrowth of his tumor, which occurred just after his last injection of dendritic vaccine. The fact that the regrowth was nowhere near his original tumor site told us that the therapies we were using in that area were working. Unfortunately, the regrowth was not operable because it was located in the midst of his short-term memory tracks. After we resumed chemotherapy with Temodar and Avastin, the new tumor began to shrink. Eventually, Mr. Tao returned to Hong Kong to be with his family. Once there, his oncologist found yet another spot in a different part of the brain, but radiation treatments were unable to control the regrowths. Glioblastoma had begun to get the upper hand; for William Tao, there would be no final "hands over head—success!"

As the aggressive tumors further infiltrated his brain, Mr. Tao became weaker and weaker. He was finally hospitalized and slipped into a coma. He is alive as I write; eighteen months after his original surgery, even in his unconscious state, the indomitable Mr. Tao still appears to be fighting for his life. "A few weeks ago, the doctors here said he only had a few days to live," his son Andrew told me. "It turns out that my father has exceeded their expectations."

Every day I am faced with the reality that the incidence of brain tumors seems to be on the rise. Recent studies suggest that the incidence of tumors is increasing particularly among seniors and children. Although it is true that we are much better now at detecting tumors than we used to be, the finding is not merely the by-product of better detection. One study suggested that the number of people with malignant primary brain tumors, like Mr. Tao's glioblastoma multiforme—tumors that originate in the brain or surrounding structures—has increased 30 to 70 percent from one decade to the next in some metropolitan areas of the United States. Beyond this figure, ten times that many metastatic brain tumors—tumors that spread to the brain from elsewhere in the body—will result from breast, colon, and lung cancers, and from melanomas.

We are learning more and more about habits and substances that may be associated with the formation of brain tumors. Although these known and suspected factors are linked to an elevated potential for brain cancer, it is important to note that a risk factor is not the same thing as a cause. We still do not know precisely why some individuals with these risk factors get cancer, while others with the same exposure do not.

I've shared my thoughts on some potential environmental dangers that may have affected Glenn Rhoades, and the risks associated with cell phone usage for patients like Tionne Watkins or my friend Johnnie Cochran. There are also risks associated with other common items that we encounter in everyday life, including pesticides, air pollution, nitrates found in cured meats, power lines, and plastics. Also high on my list of brain tumor risk factors are X-rays. We know from reported cases that X-rays can cause cancer. Radiation is associated with the development of meningiomas. The overuse of dental X-rays, particularly their frequent use in children undergoing orthodontia, concerns me. Although X-rays may be an important diagnostic tool in medical and dental care, dental X-rays are aimed not just at the jaw but at the lower brain. Because we know that X-rays can induce brain tumors, dental X-rays should be minimized. Every time I go to the dentist I am asked if I want to have my teeth x-rayed, and I routinely refuse. I haven't had a dental X-ray in twenty years.

Why me? This is often the question that many people ask after being told they have a brain tumor. It's a natural reaction, and one that I try to help my patients through with a combination of sympathy and an optimistic approach to treatment. On the other hand, as actor Michael J. Fox said after being diagnosed with Parkinson's disease, *Why not me?* Some people, because of their individual genetics, are more predisposed than others to form tumors when environmental and other factors set up the sequence of events that might initiate them. If you have the right (or wrong) genetic setup, and you are exposed to carcinogens in the environment, you may develop a tumor. In recent years we've discovered a lot about how brain tumors and cancers arise in the body, and we have developed some compelling and useful theories about their causes. Understanding the causes—in particular the chemical and biological pathways involved in the development of these tumors—will, we hope, one day enable us to find the cure.

The development of brain tumors, like tumors elsewhere in the body, has been described as a "signaling failure" within the cells. We know that in tumor formation, the normal life-death cycle of the cells becomes interrupted somewhere along the line. Cells that are genetically programmed to self-destruct at a certain point fail to enter the normal death cycle—somehow they don't get the signal. Instead they become immortal cells, forming a rogue colony with one purpose: to survive and multiply. In malignant brain tumors, these immortal cancer cells break off from the main tumor and then migrate to other parts of the brain, forming new tumor colonies. We are just now beginning to understand the nature of this process, and with each new discovery in the lab, we are developing new theories and treatment strategies to interrupt this progression at the molecular level. The dendritic vaccine we gave to Glenn Rhoades and William Tao and improved drug therapies such as Temodar and Avastin are just the beginning. Promising new treatments involving the use of microwave waves, gene-transporting herpes virus, and even radioactive scorpion venom are on the horizon.

One of the most exciting developments in cancer research is the discovery of the cancer stem cell. Within the body, stem cells are primitive, undifferentiated cells that evolve into heart cells, lung cells, brain cells, and other kinds of cells specific to our body's various organs. From our earliest moments until the moment we die, stem cells are hard at work, replenishing our dying cells with new ones. The cancer stem cell, it seems, functions in much the same way, enabling the tumor to grow by populating it with new cells.

This means that a malignant brain tumor is dependent

on cancer stem cells to survive and expand. We now believe that very few of the cells in a cancer can replicate themselves for long periods of time. Approximately 95 to 97 percent of the cells in a tumor are not cancer stem cells, and can divide only a few times before dying out.

In a way, cancer stem cells play the same role as the queen termite in a termite colony. Only the cancer stem cell—the queen termite—produces significant numbers of new tumor cells. These stem cells make up only 2 to 5 percent of all cells in the cancer, but they drive tumor growth, much like the queen termite reproduces to expand her colony. The key to finding a cure for cancer may be to focus on killing cancer stem cells. As in nature, if you want to get rid of the colony, you have to go after the queen.

Researchers in Canada first discovered cancer stem cells in 1997. The first cancer stem cells to be identified were those of leukemia, but additional studies documented the existence of stem cells in other types of cancers. At Cedars-Sinai we have isolated stem cells in glioblastoma tumors. This discovery may have far-reaching implications. If we can knock out the cancer stem cell, which, like the queen termite, is responsible for replenishing the tumor cell line, we believe we can stop the tumor from growing. Toward that end we are starting to work on development of a brain tumor vaccine that will go after cancer stem cells. Our conference call with the FDA to start a new clinical trial with a vaccine against brain cancer stem cells went well, and we hope to have approval to treat our first patient with this new vaccine shortly.

Meanwhile, the war goes on. We fight brain tumor battles on a daily basis, but one day we will win the war. That is something I *have* to believe. It's one reason I keep fighting. The other reason, of course, is my patients.

Tionne Watkins returned to Los Angeles about three months after her surgery for another follow-up visit.

"Can I have a hug?" she asked, moving toward me. "I'm a hug type of a girl."

There were warm and heartfelt hugs all around. I was delighted to see her in such high spirits. "So," I said, "how are you doing?"

"I feel really good," Tionne replied.

"Now . . . let's see you smile," I said. She turned the corners of her mouth up slightly. "No . . . not like that . . . *Really* big."

Tionne flashed me a Grammy-winning, million-megawatt, ear-to-ear grin. It was absolutely symmetrical.

"Excellent! How's your hearing?"

"Hearing is good," she said.

"Well, you're doing very well, everything looks great," I replied. "We'll see you again in three months. Okay?"

"Great," Tionne replied. I had one foot out the door when she added, "Dr. Black . . . I have to tell you what an extraordinary experience this has been. I was terrified coming out to Los Angeles, but from the moment I got here, I just knew this was where I was supposed to be. I came out totally perfect, and I don't think it would have turned out this well anywhere else. I prayed over it, my pastor did, and so did my family . . . And the day I went down to have surgery, that's the only peace I've ever had in my life, where I felt like I was going to be okay. And there's nothing better than going into surgery and not being afraid of who's going to touch you."

"Thank you," I said. "That's a wonderful compliment." I allowed myself a small moment of satisfaction for good work on behalf of a very courageous and very determined young woman.

It was yet another reminder that my patients fight their disease with the greatest dignity and spirit one can ever imagine. Their courage inspires me to focus every drop of energy I have in myself to provide them with the best odds possible to beat this disease, or at least give them as much quality life as our surgeries and medicines will allow. They are my heroes, and I hope one day all of their bravery and determination will help lead to a cure.

ACKNOWLEDGMENTS

A special thanks to Diana Baroni, who went above and beyond her duties as executive editor in the effort she spent editing this book to ensure its success. To Digby and Kay Diehl for their editorial assistance. To my agent, Frank Weimann, who believed in this project from the beginning. To everyone at Grand Central Publishing who had a hand in making the book possible, especially Les Pockell, Jamie Raab, Matthew Ballast, and Linda Duggins. And to three special people on my staff, Felicia Mayes, Teresita Casipe-Bellon, and Suzane Brian. Finally, I wish to thank Arnold Mann for helping me bring the science and patient stories in these pages to life.

ABOUT THE AUTHOR

DR. KEITH L. BLACK serves as chairman of the department of neurosurgery and director of the Maxine Dunitz Neurosurgical Institute at Cedars-Sinai Medical Center. An internationally renowned neurosurgeon and scientist, Dr. Black joined Cedars-Sinai Medical Center in July 1997 and was awarded the Ruth and Lawrence Harvey Chair in neurosciences in November of that year.

Prior to joining Cedars-Sinai, Dr. Black served on the University of California, Los Angeles, faculty for ten years as professor of neurosurgery. In 1992 he was awarded the Ruth and Raymond Stotter Chair in the department of surgery and was head of the UCLA Comprehensive Brain Tumor Program.

Dr. Black pioneered research on designing ways to open the blood-brain barrier, enabling chemotherapeutic drugs to be delivered directly into the tumor. His work in this field received the Jacob Javits award from the National Advisory Neurological Disorders and Stroke Council of the National Institutes of Health in June 2000. Dr. Black and patients undergoing the first clinical trials of the drug, RMP-7, were profiled in 1996 on the PBS program *The*

New Explorers, in an episode called "Outsmarting the Brain." His other groundbreaking research has focused on developing a vaccine to enhance the body's immune response to brain tumors, use of gene arrays to develop molecular profiles of tumors, the use of optical technology for brain mapping, and the use of focused microwave energy to noninvasively destroy brain tumors.

Dr. Black has an extraordinary ability to combine cutting-edge research and an extremely busy surgical practice. Since 1987, he has performed more than 5,000 operations for resection of brain tumors.

Dr. Black completed both his undergraduate and medical degrees at the University of Michigan in six years. He completed his internship in general surgery and residency in neurological surgery at the University of Michigan Medical Center in Ann Arbor.